# Table c

# Courageou$ Money™

# Your Adventure Through

# Money National Park™

*Changing the way we talk about money...*

*One story at a time.*

## Amy Zehnder and Cindy Coe

**AMY ZEHNDER AND CINDY COE**

Courageous Money™

Your Adventure Through

Money National Park™

# Dedication

To our sisters.

# Foreword By "The Moneyist," Quentin Fottrell

If your life was a movie, how would you like it to end?

"Comfortably" is not a bad answer. "Happily," is another acceptable one. We want to avoid "ominously" or "dramatically." You don't want an ending where you wonder, "I have no idea what's going to happen next!" We should all get to choose the ending we deserve, and we do choose it — with every small and big decision we make. The trick as a good writer/director is to make smart decisions to lead us to that Hollywood ending. If we can't imagine the ending we deserve perhaps we have not realized what is at stake. For that, we must start at the beginning.

Amy Zehnder and Cindy Coe's book *Courageou$ Money: Your Adventure Through Money National Park,* does just that by getting us to think differently about our own journey. They are the producers of the movie they would like *you*, the reader, to write and direct. This book is entertaining and informative sure, but like all good movies it has a bigger, more important message. Zehnder and Coe want you to learn more about *why* we do the things we do, and what we can learn from them. They also caution us to beware of the many traps that lie ahead.

It sounds like an easy task in principle, but it's not. It's the same problem faced by many financial advisors. How can you encourage people to save wisely and spend judiciously to create an ending that has yet to happen? It's hard to prove a counterfactual. Most people in their 30s can't fathom what they will even look like in their 40s or 50s, so how can we expect them to imagine a life beyond their wildest dreams? A future where they live in the moment *and* put enough money aside so they can enjoy a retirement free from worry and regret?

In order to enter Money National Park, you must answer this question: *What three things come to mind when you think about money?* Your answer will not only reveal your ambitions for the future, but also give valuable insights into your past. For me, these three words come to mind: Work. Freedom. Safety.

## COURAGEOUS MONEY: YOUR ADVENTURE THROUGH MONEY NATIONAL PARK

Most of us need to earn money in a way that, hopefully, fulfills us. That money should bring us freedom to go places and meet people, and put a roof over our head and food on the table. It should, if we start planning now, also bring peace of mind.

To help break free of all of fears — because we all have them — and realize our own power, Zehnder and Coe take readers on a journey through the Fountain of Youth, Gender Mountain, Generation Trail, Tall Tales Campground, and other hotspots to challenge us to think about who we are *and* who we want to be. This book helped me examine the origins of my own attitude toward money, and how everything we do is in turn affected by it. Every financial advisor, psychologist and therapist in the country should visit Money National Park. And so should you.

*Quentin Fottrell is the Moneyist advice columnist, advising readers on the ethics and etiquette of their financial affairs, and the Personal Finance Editor for MarketWatch.*

# Introduction to Courageou$ Money

*"Money is a terrible master but an excellent servant." ~P.T. Barnum*

"Original, intriguing, uproarious, and riveting," were the words used by the critics to describe the action-adventure movie titled, *Courageous Money: Your Adventure Through Money National Park*, a story depicting a life-long relationship with money from early childhood through adulthood. With similarities to *Raiders of the Lost Ark* or Lara Croft's *Tomb Raider*, *Courageous Money* is filled with both triumphant moments and dangerous, cliff-hanging scenes. In fact, *Courageous Money* may be the most compelling movie that you have ever seen. Why? Because this adventure-movie is based on *your* story—The story of your personal relationship with money. You play the main character!

The movie begins with your childhood and follows you to the present. The plot is focused on your journey to fulfill your dreams and passions, all the while navigating endless courageous money challenges and victories.

There seems to be a never-ending pursuit of money and the thought of being rich in today's world. The idea of being rich permeates Hollywood and our media experiences. Consider for example the sheer number of movies with plots about searching for lost treasure, winning the lottery, or hitting the jackpot in Vegas. If a poll was taken today with a box for, "I want to be rich," would you check the box? What if there was a price to pay for being rich? Would you want to know that price before saying yes to your riches?

Whether or not you realize it, you are already playing this money game, balancing risk and reward with your time and efforts, in every decision you make, regardless of your financial circumstances and net worth.

There is a universal assumption that money can buy happiness and the more money you have, the happier you will be. The truth is, money *does* make us happier, but only to a certain extent. A 2018 Purdue University study used data from the Gallup World Poll and found that those interviewed said the "ideal" annual income point for individuals is $95,000 *for life satisfaction*, yet only

# COURAGEOUS MONEY: YOUR ADVENTURE THROUGH MONEY NATIONAL PARK

$60,000 to $75,000 was actually needed for *emotional well-being*. When people earned more than $105,000, believe it or not their happiness levels *decreased*. In the future, experts say that the amount of money needed for happiness will remain around the median income for U.S. residents, which in 2021 is $63,179.

If money doesn't buy happiness, why have so many people dedicated and, in some cases, lost their lives searching for ancient treasures, gold, or the promised land? Why are there so many stories and movies about striking it rich, trading self-worth for money (*Indecent Proposal*), or making it big and winning the lottery? In the working world, people sacrifice their health and even their family relationships to make money and, in the end, sacrifice that money to preserve their health and longevity. The Dalai Lama, when asked what surprised him most about humanity, answered, "Man! Because he sacrifices his health in order to make money. Then he sacrifices money to recuperate his health. And then he is so anxious about the future that he does not enjoy the present; the result being that he does not live in the present or the future; he lives as if he is never going to die, and then dies having never really lived."

This paradox runs deep within us. At an early age, earlier than you think, we develop a relationship with money that controls the majority of our behaviors, actions, and choices as adults. For some, this relationship with money is love-hate, for others it is a life-long dance. Be it a waltz, 2-step, hip-hop or free form, money controls us!

Despite this strong connection to money, it remains the number one taboo topic of conversation within households worldwide. In the recent past, the two biggest conversations avoided in homes were sex and money. Nowadays, parents find it easier to talk to their kids about sex than about money!

When money is discussed at home it is often at a surface level (focused on immediate spending needs), instead of being purposefully focused on financial education or financial strategies such as budgeting, planning, savings, investing, or what a money request means to the family's larger financial picture. For example, Presha (a teenager) may need $40 to go to the movies and have pizza with her friends but has no idea that when her Mother says, "No," it's because that money is not in the family budget for that month. Nor does she know what unexpected expenses have come up for the family that have already impacted their monthly budget. Presha hears only "No," while her mom lives with guilt for not giving her daughter what she wants, but never explaining "why." Consider the difference if Presha was involved in the monthly budget and was able to help the family manage to it. This would be a far reach for most households to operate this way, but think of the difference it could make.

Given that money "makes the world go around," and drives so many of our behaviors, it is astounding to consider that the topic of money is dormant in most homes. Our relationship with money is deeply-rooted within us and similar to the relationship we have with other personal items such as our phone, watch, jewelry, car, hair, clothes and house; it often defines us.

So, if money is such a big factor in our lives, then why don't we talk about it? Simply stated, we don't know *how*. Our parents didn't discuss it openly; our friends, siblings, work colleagues and extended family members don't discuss it either. When it comes to money conversations, there are few good role-models to follow. With Courageous Money, we hope to change that.

Somewhere in our past, we've all experienced or witnessed the "Hush!" story; when a young child blurts out at the holiday dinner table, "Uncle Albert, how much money do you make?" and the stunned family goes silent and red-faced until someone speaks up and corrects the child by saying, "Hush honey, it's impolite to ask people about money or how much they make." With that response, the money conversation is forever over. It is buried, never to be discussed again, and we carry that "hush" programming with us for life.

Money stories don't always have to be about dollars and cents! Too often, people think when we say "money conversations," we are asking you to share amounts, bank balances, salaries, net worth, finances or lack thereof. Sometimes this may be appropriate, but often it's not necessary.

To make matters worse, money conversations have become even more non-existent because money is no longer tangible. Gone are the paper and coin that we held in our hands; money is now *invisible*! Consequently, what was rarely discussed in the past became even more intangible. How can we perceive or discuss that which is invisible?

There is one source that keeps money, even invisible money stories, alive and in the public eye. Who better to give us fodder to talk about money than Hollywood? From the early years of filmmaking, Hollywood has been telling money stories: Rags to riches, the gold rush, lottery winning, hitting the jackpot, searching for hidden treasure, playing the stock market, cheating the stock market, and being flat broke and down on your luck stories about every money situation you can imagine. Perhaps some of these movie titles will jog your memory of how money was portrayed.

> *The Lucky Texan* (1934), *It's a Wonderful Life* (1946), *Tycoon* (1947), *Treasure of the Sierra Madre* (1948), *Giant* (1956), *Willy Wonka and the Chocolate Factory* (1964), *Trading Places* (1983), *A Christmas Carol* (1984), *Goonies* (1985), *Wall Street* (1987), *Strike it Rich* (1990), *Pretty Woman* (1990), *It Could Happen to You* (1994), *Blank Check* (1994), *Jerry Maguire* (1996), *Catch Me if You Can* (2002), *Maid in Manhattan* (2002), *The Pursuit of Happiness* (2006), *Slumdog Millionaire* (2009), *Lottery Ticket* (2010), *Nina's Dowry* (2012), *Internship* (2013), *The Wolf of Wall Street* (2013), *Schitt's Creek* (2105), *Gold* (2016), *Molly's Game* (2017), *Knives Out* (2019), *Parasite* (2019) and *Minari* (2020)

These films and many others have done a great job of portraying the history of money and showing how currency was used for the survival and evolution of humankind. While cultural norms have ensured the unacceptable nature of speaking about money in anything other than an "in exchange for" perspective (think of a woman's dowry and the stock exchange), films have kept a variety of money themes front and center. Suffice it to say, they have conducted many of our money conversations for us.

The most recent focus in the financial services industry has been on women, especially women in wealth, due to the significant amount of wealth being created by and inherited by women; thank you Oprah Winfrey, Arianna Huffington, Mackenzie Bezos, Celine Dion, Ellen DeGeneres, Zhong Huijuan,

Julia Koch, Alice Walton, Jacqueline Mars, and the Williams sisters, among others. Couple this with rising generations learning about money through their smart devices, and the time to start talking about our relationship with money is *now*! Where do we start that conversation? Right here.

Money is rarely explored in terms of the emotional relationship we have with it, or what we call the *psychology of money*. We don't consciously think about or discuss how money is connected to our upbringing, zip code, culture, religion, socioeconomics, gender, generation, birth order, family systems and temperament (the character traits we are born with). We don't think about how our job and education choices, as well as our interpersonal relationships at home and at work, relate to our *money messages*. We also don't take the time to discover the money messages we learned at an early age that have/will carry us into adulthood. Believe it or not, these messages culminate in volumes of stories related to our lives and are foundational to our behaviors and decisions.

If you were to consciously turn your life lessons about money into an action-adventure movie, what plot-lines, stories and lessons would emerge? As with every compelling story, we want a happy ending! With money as the main character the ending could be a surprise. Is your movie a romance, comedy, or action-adventure? Maybe it's hair-raising suspense drama, or thriller! Horror? Let's not go there!

What will your money movie look like? What will it model for the next generation—who, by the way, rarely interact with tangible (paper/coin) money or see real money exchange hands anymore? What are your favorite money movie scenes? If you are like most people, when first asked to tell your money stories, you may not know exactly what to share. Or, you might recall a few but not enough to create a movie... That's where *Courageou$ Money* comes in.

You are about to embark on an adventure that will help you recall your stories and create your money-adventure movie! Your movie will include scenes about the *where* and *how* you were raised, your siblings influence, your first job, and your core beliefs about money and so much more. But before you start this journey, it is important that you have a better understanding of what is meant by money stories, money messages, money mindsets and just how deeply-rooted money is to your values and emotions. We also included a brief section designed to encourage those who believe that they are not financially savvy enough, to step into this space.

Courageous Money isn't about *how much* money you have, it's about what it means to you.

# PART I. DEMYSTIFYING MONEY MESSAGES

*"Fortune favors the bold." ~ Turnus, Roman goddess*

# What's the Message?

We all have a relationship with money. Your adult behavior concerning your personal relationship with money is driven by the money messages you learned in your formative years. Lessons that came from a culmination of upbringing, culture, gender, generation, and temperament, just to name a few. Messages that you have adopted as part of your belief-system, which have guided your behaviors into adulthood. What you observed and experienced as a young child formulated your views of money, which now guide the majority of your behaviors and decisions as an adult. Yes, it's true! In doing the research and interviews for this book, we were astounded at the number of people who immediately saw these connections once they began to share their money stories.

# Mountains of Money Messages

What are *money messages*? Thoughts and beliefs about money that are so deeply rooted that you often don't consider them to be the source or drivers of your actions and behaviors. For example, when we see a young girl in her early twenties spending a lot of money, rarely do we associate her spending habits with her values, temperament, money mindset or her money messages—Lessons adopted from her earliest memories of money. Instead, we would attribute her spending to stereotypes and more observable attributes such as her youth or gender. We would make assessments such as: "She spends like a girl without any responsibilities." "She's young and doesn't know the value of money." Or "All women are shoppers!" In this example, it's easy to see the obvious (she's young and female, and culturally we associate both with spending/shopping). What we rarely factor into our assessment is people's values, money mindset and early money messages. We typically would not consider perspectives such as: this young lady's top value is personal freedom, her money mindset is that of a 'spender' and her money message learned at an early age was, "If you earn your own money, you can buy your own things."

You may have noticed that we've mentioned both *money mindset* and *money messages*. Is there a difference? Yes. *Money Mindsets* are tied to both your temperament and your values. There are four money mindsets (Saver, Spender, Investor and Giver) that you will learn more about when you start to create your money movie in Part II of this book. *Money Messages*, on the other hand, are statements, sayings, perspectives, communications, quotes or self-talk that you have adopted as part of your beliefs; for argument's sake, some stereotypical money messages may include:

1. I don't need to worry about money, money has always been there for me, so I know that it will always be there for me.
2. I work hard for money and to have more, I need to work more.
3. I must be the sole provider for others; they need me for my ability to provide.
4. No matter how hard I work, I will always be behind when it comes to

money.

5. I never trust anyone but myself, because in an instant it could all be gone or inaccessible to me. (Reality Check: This belief can come from having experienced a tragic loss: divorce, death, parents' divorce, business closing or economic crisis.)

6. Men should make more money than women.

7. My spouse/partner is smart, and I trust them with our finances, so I don't need to know anything about it, unless I'm forced into it someday. (Reality Check: Many women will end up managing household finances, especially in their senior years.)

8. Someone will take care of me, so I don't need to get a degree or make my own money. (Reality Check: This has been said by a few women of a certain generation, joking that they went to college to get their "Mrs." degree/find a husband.)

9. Others will see my good work and reward me for it. (Reality Check: You need to be your own advocate or cheerleader for raises, promotions, and/or starting salary at a new job.)

10. I'm just happy to have this job. It would be nice if they paid me more, but I'm not going to ask for it.

11. I can't apply for a job if I don't meet all of the qualifications listed. (Reality Check: Women often doubt themselves more than men and therefore take less risks when applying for jobs or career advancements. Women are also more willing to settle for less money because they are happy to have any opportunity.)

12. I have money right now; I'll worry about where to get more later.

13. I don't have enough money to start that fancy investing stuff. (Reality Check: Women often doubt themselves more than men and therefore take less risks when investing. But when they do invest, they often make more. They also start investing later than men, according to a U.S. Bank Wealth Management study.)

14. I have enough to take care of the basics for my family and that's plenty.

15. A women's place is still in the home. (Reality Check: Women often take on most of the household chores in addition to working outside the home. According to Melinda Gates in her book The Power of

Lift, women in the U.S. spend on average, ninety minutes per day more than men on unpaid work (cooking, cleaning, childcare, household work) which equates to about seven years more of unpaid work compared to men. This statistic is significantly greater in less developed countries.)

16. If I am not the primary breadwinner, I have to contribute in other ways to make up the difference. (Reality Check: Money is not the only form of currency.)

17. I will never have enough money to retire without worry.

Can you relate to any of these statements? This is where we begin to recognize and examine not only the money messages we carry, but also how they impact our lives and families. You get to decide what you want to do with this information. For instance, is there a self-limiting belief here that you want to address?

Our goal with this book is to provide you with insight. Engaging with this book can change the way you view your personal money habits and reveal what storyline might be emerging for your money movie. As you move forward, you will learn more about what money messages are and how they have shaped your world. We also encourage you to have this a dialogue with others. By sharing your stories with one another, you can understand and change the hypnotic power that money has over you. Our contributors ("Explorers") in this book, were astounded at the revelations they came to about money in just an hour interview; and how much dialogue it sparked within their families.

# Money See, Money Do

Keep in mind that sometimes our ingrained money messages can also be self-defeating. Thus, we will want you to examine your money messages for them to become conscious choices that serve you in positive, productive ways. With this consciousness, you will also be free to release some long-held beliefs that are no longer serving you. Some beliefs that were planted by your family of origin perhaps; some knowingly, many unknowingly, as well as those rooted many generations before you even took your first breath! According to Bowen's Family Systems Theory and Lieberman's Transgenerational Theory, family patterns repeat through generations, specific practices, behaviors and beliefs reappear and any family dynamic is subject to being re-enacted. Deeply embedded in these repeating patterns are practices, behaviors and beliefs about money.

Regardless of where your money messages came from, you will have the opportunity to consciously affirm, revise or eliminate them as your own. Set yourself free by releasing those that no longer serve you and embrace the new.

# When Money Talks

Our tagline for this book is, "Changing the way we talk about money...One story at a time." *Money stories* are ways to start talking about money. Money is complex and our relationship with money is equally so. Money is deeply tied to our emotions and core values. Think about what happens when you experience a loss of income (demotion, job termination), loss of net worth (market volatility, bad investments), or even the thought of lost or reduced income (retirement, divorce); if you have a core value of freedom for example, such losses elicit a feeling of fear because you perceive that you may no longer be free to do what you want, when you want. What you were counting on financially may not be there anymore—Even the perception of diminished freedom elicits fear. If security and family are your core values and you have spent years earning money to take care of your family, when something happens that impacts your income or nest egg, it messes with your value of security. This then elicits emotions to surface such as guilt, anger, and disappointment because you tell yourself that you should have planned better or sacrificed more. This is why market volatility hits people so hard; it hits them at their core, it shakes their relationship with money because it shakes their values system—sometimes people sell out in panic.

Money has more control over us than we want to admit, and it aligns with more emotions than people realize. For example, shame and guilt have a direct relationship to money; if people have too much, they feel ashamed or guilty. If they have too little, they feel ashamed or guilty. Beyond shame and guilt, money is connected to our deepest, primal emotions of love, joy, fear, and anger. Money is also directly correlated to our need for certainty; the greater the level of financial uncertainty, e.g., market volatility, the greater the fear. You cannot disconnect your relationship with money from these emotions. You simply need to be aware of how money sparks these emotions and consequential behaviors, and find ways to become harmonious with them or use them to thrive.

Throughout our lives, money helps weave the narrative about our personal and professional lives and controls our choices and behaviors, thus, creating what we call your personal "money movie". Typically, this movie stays within your mind, only to be seen by you. Yet, as with all movies, plots change quickly and take unexpected turns. Therefore, it is imperative that you learn to share your money stories, as the protagonist in your money movie. When you share your story out loud, you may see things differently. You may discover solutions that you had not thought of before and just as importantly, others learn, too.

As you create your *Courageous Money* movie, you will learn more about how to share your stories and get more comfortable talking about money. Along the way, you might realize that it gets easier to lead uncomfortable money conversations, and you may begin to feel more comfortable including the "dollars and cents" we mentioned earlier. Money-oriented narratives are about having a holistically healthy financial life, also known as your 'financial wellness'. You can't have financial wellness without understanding the motivations behind your money habits. This is why dialogue is paramount!

Many were forced to have conversations about money during the COVID-19 (Coronavirus) pandemic. Besides choosing whose turn it was to mask-up and brave the grocery store or where to find the elusive toilet paper, people began to talk more openly with family members and employers about their financial reserves (or lack thereof), income vs. debt, as well as what the pandemic meant for current and future income sources; not just in 2020 but in the coming years as well. They did so because they had to. Because for the first time in many families there were conversations about scarcity and limits. For far too many other families, scarcity is all they'd ever known and that reality became indisputable during the pandemic, which meant not being able to pay for a roof over their head or buy food, something that was always priority one. In some cases, other family members found ways to help out (E.g., teenagers got jobs), but it required a *money conversation.*

For those with enough to give, it surfaced conversations about altruism; where and how to help others in need. COVID gave a new meaning to "money talks," it forced the world to talk about money. Although most of us are still not good at it.

# Understanding the Movie in Your Mind

Hopefully it is becoming easier to see how money affects people's lives across the board: From child-rearing methods to interacting and communicating with others, leading, managing, political and social behaviors, to how people define their educational and career choices. This book is designed to help you demystify the powerful, controlling influences that money has on you and identify where your money messages come from; only then can you decide if they are (still) serving you.

We have decided to take a creative approach to this serious topic by asking you to turn your money story into a movie. We hope that you will find enjoyment in the process and that it will inspire others to join in on your adventure; bringing people closer together and ultimately enlightening everyone to more conscious choices. There is power in sharing your stories, and as a result, everyone can make more conscious choices. Storytelling creates a collaborative movement. *The Health Foundation UK*, in their article "The Power of Storytelling," tells us that:

> Storytelling gives us an opportunity to learn from another person's experience and it can shape, strengthen or challenge our opinions and values. When a story catches our attention and engages us, we are more likely to absorb the message and meaning within it than if the same message was presented simply in facts and figures. When someone tells us their own personal story, we catch a glimpse of a view of the world that may be slightly or radically different from our own. When we see the world as they see it, or walk in their shoes, the experience can inspire empathy...

*Courageou$ Money: Your Adventure Through Money National Park* is designed to help you capture your personal *Courageous Money* movie. To accomplish this task, you will visit various stops in *Money National Park*. Each stop is specifically designed to help you see/create more of your movie. By the time you reach the end, your movie will reveal your personal relationship with money. While on the journey, you will discover the who, what, where, when and why of your money messages and how they impact your life. The happy ending will be your invitation to choose only those money messages that will continue to serve you going forward.

While all are welcome on this adventure, we want anyone resisting the financial side of their world to venture into this space with the guarantee that you will find value in thinking about your money messages, editing them, adding new insight to your money narrative, and relaxing into what might be a different routine for your money management. In reality, *all* of our routines link to our relationship with money.

As you think back to share the stories that make up your movie, you will have a lot to draw from. And, if you are reading this book alongside others (even if you live together), each person may see these stories (movie scenes) from different perspectives. The beautiful part of this adventure is if you open yourself up to hearing other's perspectives of the same scene, event, or situation, you might see things differently or gain new insight.

You might be familiar with the book, *The Four Agreements* by Don Miguel Ruiz. The second agreement, "Don't Take Things Personally," uses a movie analogy to describe how our reality is different from other's realities and how we can change our perspective of our movie script. After all, the way you see your movie is according to the agreements that you have with yourself and you have the power to change these agreements. Here is an excerpt from the book:

> Imagine that you are in a gigantic mall where there are hundreds of movie theaters. You look around to see what's playing, and you notice a movie that has your name. Amazing! You go inside the theater, and it's empty except for one person. Very quietly, trying not to interrupt, you sit behind that person, who doesn't even notice you; all that person's attention is on the movie.
>
> You look at the screen, and what a big surprise! You recognize every character in the movie—your mother, your father, your brothers and sisters, your beloved, your children, your friends. Then you see the main character of the movie, and it's you! You are the star of the

movie and it's the story of you. And that person in front of you, well, it's also you, watching yourself act in the movie. Of course, the main character is just the way you believe you are, and so are all the secondary characters because you know the story of you. You decide to go to another theater.

In this theater, there is also just one person watching a movie, and she doesn't even notice when you sit beside her. You start watching the movie, and you recognize all the characters, but now you're just a secondary character. This is the story of your mother's life, and she is the one who is watching the movie with all her attention. ...The way she projects herself is completely different in her movie. It's the way your mother wants everyone to perceive her. You know that it's not authentic. She's just acting. But then you begin to realize that it's the way she perceives herself, and it's kind of a shock.

Then you notice that the character who has your face is not the same person who was in your movie. You say to yourself, "Ah, this isn't me," but now you can see how your mother perceives you, what she believes about you, and it's far from what you believe about yourself...

You go to the next theater, and it's the story of your beloved. Now you can see the way your beloved perceives you, and the character is completely different from the one who was in your movie and the one who was in your mother's movie. ...After seeing all these movies, you decide to return to the first theater to see your own movie once again. You look at yourself acting in your movie, but you no longer believe anything you're watching; you no longer believe your own story because you can see that it's just a story. Now you know that all the acting you did your whole life was really for nothing because nobody perceives you the way you want to be perceived.

The point of this excerpt for our purposes, is to illustrate that everyone sees their movie differently—each person perceives themselves differently than they are perceived by others—which is why it's important to share your money movies with one another and seek understanding from varying perspectives.

With the addition of Ruiz's 5th agreement, "Be Skeptical, But Learn to Listen," one blogger stated, "With few exceptions, everyone's movie is a very distorted version of reality, including yours. So be skeptical. But as pieces of art, each individual's movie reveals a lot about where they are coming from and what kind of mental box they have put themselves in. So, it pays to listen in order to understand."

What do you need to listen to in order to understand where you are coming from regarding your movie? Going back to the original premise of this book, stating that "the majority of our behaviors as an adult are rooted in our earliest memories of when and how we learned the value of money," what do you need to listen to and what boxes have you put yourself in? What would you see if you were watching your movie about how money plays a role in your life? Could this book premise be true for you? In your movie, do you have the courage to talk about money? Do you have the courage to change old habits and forge new ones? Are you courageous enough to talk to your children, parents and partners (romantic and business) about money and/or share your money movie scenes with them? More importantly, *do you know how*? That's what this adventure is all about!

# Finding Your Courage in Finance

Before you start your journey through Money National Park, it is extremely important to address the origins of *Courageous Money*. We the authors, Amy and Cindy, have years of experience in the financial service industry. We see the writing on the wall with certain demographics not taking the initiative to become financially savvy; most commonly women of older generations. We also see the *lack* of financial skills being taught to the younger generations. Basic financial skills that used to be taught in schools or from the family's local banker, store or lemonade stand are no longer being taught. As the dollar became more invisible in the Digital Age, so did the teachings. When we asked people from older generations where they learned basic financial skills, such as how to use checking and saving accounts, they would reply, "From my family's local banker." When asked who taught them how to count back change (now an almost obsolete skill), it was often a parent, a garage sale or a job as a store cashier (before those fancy computer-cash registers).

Who is teaching the kids of today about how money flows into and through households? Not just the *value of money*, but how it all works: spending, saving, investing, tracking and giving! If money is invisible, and what is invisible is challenging to manage or master; and talking about money is taboo, this is a dangerous combination with long-term negative implications!

One encouraging piece of the equation is that younger generations who *choose* to learn about money have a lot of access to this knowledge within the palm of their hands (smart phones). The amount of financial information available online these days is endless, and yet some people may not know where to start their learning process. If you want to know where to start or how to become more financially savvy, this short section applies to you:

1.  Whether or not you are the primary financial wiz in your family, start by knowing the log-in codes to all of your banking and investing accounts (and have a different, uber secure, safely stored password, for each account).
2.  Identify what it costs to live your lifestyle (this means creating a

budget, even at a high level, that highlights both incoming funds and outgoing expenses on a weekly/monthly and/or annual basis). Create your budget on paper, in Excel or using our favorite phone/computer app: YNAB (You Need a Budget).

3. Learn about saving and investing by researching basic information on saving platforms such as a 401K, IRA, Roth IRA, Roth 401K (if available), Simple IRA (for entrepreneurs) and investment terms such as stocks, bonds, diversified portfolio, dividends, mutual funds and ETFs (electronically traded funds).

4. Learn about credit card interest and how much a single purchase will cost you if you only pay the minimum payment (a $1,000 purchase could take over 30 years to pay off). Pull your free credit reports every calendar year from each of the big three (3) credit bureaus to check for open/closed accounts and fraud. The three are Equifax, Trans Union and Experian. Take it one step further by learning about credit scores and how much they impact your purchasing power (missing a house payment has the biggest hit on your credit score next to a bankruptcy, and shopping for credit can also reduce your credit score).

5. If any of these suggestions left you thinking, "Huh?" find a way to educate yourself or find a mentor who can help!

As authors, we don't profess to be financial planning experts. Amy is a wealth/financial psychologist and money coach working in the financial services sector and with families, and Cindy has been coaching families and family-owned businesses for years. Thus, we have a working knowledge of how the pieces of Spending, Saving, Investing and Giving fit together. In our work, we focus on the emotional side of money.

We are also privileged to work with the most amazing finance and estate planning attorney, Cynthia Tremaroli, J.D. In her work she sees the value of having these conversations and the consequences of not. We asked Cynthia what advice she would give:

As early as possible create a life plan, a plan that involves the financial pieces of the picture. Find a way to balance living life with your pursuit of money so that neither consume you. And, don't use money to buy behaviors, such as love and friendships.

Get involved! As a child my dad would come home at the end of the week with his barber shop earnings. I wanted to know the details! I wanted to know 'how much' so that we, as a family, could help decide how much to save and how much to spend on food. By knowing the details, we were all invested in working within our family budget. There were four kids by now and we had to figure this out. Not all kids are capable of being involved, but for those who are, even at a young age, let them be part of the solution. Share the details when and if possible. If, for any reason, it's not suitable to share your financial details with your kids, at the very least, teach them what *not* to do.

# Money Confidence

In terms of *money confidence*, let it be known that there are three things that money cannot buy: self-confidence, self-esteem, and self-worth!

Self-confidence is a measure of one's own abilities; self-esteem focuses on our sense of self—what we think, feel and believe about our self, and self-worth is knowing that we are of value—both loveable and necessary. Some people can possess good self-esteem, but lack self-confidence, while others possess strong self-confidence but lack self-esteem. We could designate a whole chapter to the relationship between these three self-assessment areas, but for the purpose of this book, the one that ties most closely to money confidence is self-confidence, thus we focus there.

Self-confidence can be situational; meaning you can be confident in one situation yet not in others. This is why many people can be very confident in some roles they have chosen for themselves, such as child rearing, household chores, gardening, breadwinner, and less confident in other roles, like financial management.

Self-confidence comes from overcoming something. A form of mastery that comes from experience and problem solving; the ability to solve a problem and overcome it, especially during a crisis. Once you have achieved something, you have gained confidence that you can do it again. Everyone should know, at some level, they have the competency (skills) to contribute to solutions and solve problems.

Money affords the perfect opportunity for building this self-confidence, and not just in saving and investing. Be willing to make mistakes. There is a difference between risk-taking and being reckless. Money confidence requires you to step into the space, take some risks, learn and distinguish, without being reckless. At the same time, your ability to step into the money space may be governed by earlier money messages and upbringing and you probably don't realize it. We will cover this a great deal in a few of our adventure scenes in Money National Park.

Confidence comes from taking risks. Because this entire book encompasses *Courageous Money*, including money stories both tragic and triumphant, here are a few brief stories about courage that we, the authors, have experienced.

# Win Some, Lose Some

"We've both made some dough and lost some dough." Our tragic money management stories can be summed up in three mistakes:

1. Amy listened to her dad's financial advisor and got involved in a whole-life insurance program, not realizing that this type of investment would require a monthly contribution for life! This was ill advice given to a college student. Amy says, "In my doctorate program, I couldn't afford a Taco Bell burrito much less pay these premiums! I stopped paying. I incurred a penalty, and needless to say, I lost my tail." Lesson learned: Do your homework, don't just take someone else's advice if it doesn't feel right.

2. Then, both of us (Amy and Cindy) invested what was then a hefty sum into a friend's business. Shortly after we made the investment, we saw some disturbing things, like him driving a new Jaguar and all of their adult kids "working" for the company! There was no ROI (return on investment) in sight. They stopped sending quarterly reports and then stopped returning calls. We hired an attorney to try to get our money back. It didn't happen. Lesson learned: Just because they are your friends, doesn't mean it's a good investment!

3. In 2003, we invested in two stocks that were both well before their time. The first, one of the original RFID companies and the second, synthetic blood. Yes, you read that right. When there is a shortage of blood supply (e.g., war, crisis), they can use the synthetic blood as a substitute. We were willing to invest in these cutting-edge inventions but alas, we were ahead of our time. Both went belly up. Both, by the way, are thriving industries today. Synthetic blood is being used in emergency rooms across the country and well, look at that little RFID chip on your credit card. The good news is we also invested in Apple! Our triumph story is that we were early investors in the very device you may be using to read this book. Thanks to Cindy, for that one! Lesson learned: Sometimes it's worth it to take a risk here and there if you can afford it; again, risk-taking, not recklessness.

Some people think that if you are fortunate enough have a financial advisor that you don't need to know about managing your finances—your advisor has you covered, end of story. Some financial advisors are wonderful, well-meaning, well-versed and inherently interested in helping people to fulfill their dreams by using money wisely. In fact, you'll meet a few in Money National Park. Others, may be predatory and make promises they can't keep. If your advisor is servicing over 800 clients, in our opinion, it will be hard to receive the individualized attention and regular advice or oversight on your investment portfolio that you deserve. We are hard on advisors and the good ones can take it! True story: Both of us moved our money away from an advisor because this person had 800 clients. We requested quarterly reviews of our financial portfolios and to be pinged when big market shifts occurred, to evaluate any proposed changes to our portfolio, which never happened. We ran into this advisor at a social event *a year later*. The advisor introduced us as a client, never realizing that we had taken our money elsewhere. Moral of story: Make your money work for you and more importantly, make others involved in your money work for you! Be an active participant in your money matters, even if you have a spouse/partner and/or advisor involved. When you don't know what you don't know, find out what you need to know and learn it!

# Till Death Do Us Part

Some advice for women in their wisdom years: If you are partnered with or married to a man, chances are, you will outlive your male counterpart. Yet, many women from older generations are hesitant to be involved with, let alone be in-charge of, the family finances unless they are forced to be involved. According to the United States Census Bureau, 80% of married women will outlive their husbands. And almost half of all widows say they wish they would have taken a more active role in their finances when their spouses were alive.

Studies show that many of these women actually fear finances and associate dreadful words with it. Women who fear financials often have numerous money messages that have keep them from getting involved in their money matters. Here are some common money messages that are adopted as personal truths. See how many might relate to you or someone you love:

- My MAN takes care of all of that for me, I don't need to.
- I don't have to.
- I don't want to.
- I know enough to get by.
- My kids will take care of it for me.
- I don't like it.
- I don't do math.
- I'm the wine expert, not the money expert.
- It's against my religion.
- I'm a traditionalist, it's not my role.
- It's not socially acceptable for the me to take care of our money.
- I can't!
- I'm not smart enough.
- I wouldn't know the first thing about it.
- I'm too old to learn.
- Someone else has always taken care of it for me.
- My role is the kids, his role is/was the money.
- What if I do it better than he does?

- He won't like that.
- He won't let me.
- Can't I hire someone for that?
- I don't have time!

Speaking of time, time is often the biggest excuse (especially by women) for not being financially savvy or involved. Somehow women find time for all the other things: kids, chores, work, errands, taking care of others, even spa/wine weekends with girlfriends but not their household finances. If this applies to you, we encourage you to dig deep, grab some courage, and get involved. However exasperated or afraid you may be, find a way to get more acquainted with money and your finances. A little knowledge will go a long way! When you say you don't have the time, what you are really saying is, it's not a priority.

This advice is not *just* for women! If you live with a strong figure (male or female) who oversees your financial world, recognize this person for their contributions (dedication, intelligence and knowledge for their efforts), then ask if they are *willing* to share the basics with you. Not that you want to take over this role, it's simply important for you to not be afraid of it. More importantly, it's essential for you to be informed and know where to go for what—because if tragedy strikes, you don't want to be floundering with finances while you are grieving or worse be taken advantage of. Ask your partner if they are willing to help you get some peace of mind now so that in the end if you are forced to get involved or be in charge of the money, that you know how.

We would encourage you to re-evaluate all of the money messages that have prevented you from getting involved because by death, divorce or by choice, especially if you are a woman married to a man, chances are you will be in charge of your finances.

# Exercise Courage

Melinda Gates, in her book, *The Power of Lift*, stated, "If you want to lift a society up, you need to stop keeping women down." We would like to adapt that statement to read, "If you want to raise yourself up, stop holding yourself down!"

In *Writing for Success,* Debra DiPetro, creator of *The Warm Milk Journal*, recommends five exercises for jumpstarting your career, which can also easily apply to your relationship with money. We think of these as exercises in courage! See if the simplicity of this short list has an impact on you:

1.  Set your compass to courage. Think of courage as your North Star or brightest star in the sky that you're aiming for when you make a decision.
2.  Face your fears. Write down a list of fears and notice how you feel. Now you know what to work on.
3.  Do what scares you. Commit to taking actions on the fears you listed. As you face and do what you are afraid of, courage builds.
4.  Embrace uncertainty. Take risks. With risk, freedom opens up other doors.
5.  Allow yourself to be vulnerable. Don't hide and keep yourself from the world.

This is a lot of information, so you may be asking yourself, where do I start? Start by completing the upcoming adventure through Money National Park! Create your money movie and see what insights emerge. Discover your history and deeper reasoning behind what is holding you back. If you have a spouse/partner, ask them to go on this journey with you, *especially* if they are currently in charge of your finances. If your spouse/partner is not a willing participant, no worries, reach out to others who would be willing to join you; be it friend, your kids, your book club, other family members or trusted advisors. And, yes, you can go it alone! It could be enlightening and life changing. Take this journey and make a new commitment to yourself to become more financially savvy.

# What Doesn't Touch On Money?

We thought it might be helpful for you to read an example of someone else's money story—a true narrative from a trained financial psychologist. In sharing her key money messages, she validated many of the concepts shared here in Part I:

Moira Somers, Ph.D., is a psychologist, professor and family wealth consultant based in Winnipeg, Manitoba. But as far as we are concerned, the only intro she needs is spot-on from her book, *Advice That Sticks*: "Here's what I've come to believe: Most people are at least mildly crazy when it comes to money. I can say 'crazy' with some authority. I am, after all, a psychologist. I know crazy when I see it. And there is nothing—not full moons or federal elections or family get-togethers—that draws the crazy out of people faster than money."

Dr. Somers has an interestingly varied career as a neuropsychologist, a professor at a medical school, and a family wealth consultant. She was gracious enough to share some of her own money messages.

> Money is interwoven into everything. What doesn't touch on money?! My understanding of money is that it developed from both implicit and explicit lessons I learned at home and elsewhere. The implicit learning happened mostly from listening to the stories my family told about everyday events ranging from purchases to trips to donations, and from the interpretive spin put on them by various people in the room. One of the explicitly taught lessons in our home was about needing to "live within one's means"—that lesson could have been embroidered on a sampler and put on the wall! My mom was ferocious about our needing to be independent and self-sufficient, and taught us that we needed to have an education and strong work ethic as a condition for having a good life.
>
> I remember being nine or ten years old, sitting at the dining room table and visiting with my brother, who had dropped out of high school much to my parents' consternation. He had brought home

his first pay stub from working on big ships on the Great Lakes. He showed my mom his pay stub and she got really quiet and said, "You had more taken out of your paycheck in taxes in one pay period than I earn in a month!" I remember being stunned by the revelation, "How could this have happened?!" My brother had broken one of the cardinal rules about needing a good education to earn great money. My money message was shattered. I knew how hard my mom worked, but I hadn't known until that moment just how little she earned from all that hard work. This event introduced a different narrative and possibility than the one I had been taught. There was evidently more to getting ahead than just being a good student, working hard, and living within one's means.

When I was growing up, there was no entrepreneurial training or teaching about investing, and no explicit guidance about needing to investigate the earning potential of any career. There was a whole world of money I didn't learn about, a whole lot of financial education I needed to get when I left home. It took courage for me to ask people what I should be learning about, and to ask for their help in teaching me. "My career as a wealth psychologist definitely came out of my clinical work as a neuropsychologist. As I worked with patients whose lives had been turned upside down by sudden accidents or serious diseases, I saw just how much their pre-existing financial habits affected their eventual health outcomes. It wasn't just a matter of how poor or rich they were at the time of the life-altering health event; it was about their pre-existing habits and skills with money and around money. Could they have frank and tender conversations with their spouse when they were financially stressed? Had they invested in disability insurance? Had they declared their pre-accident income honestly so that, when it was time to get insurance payments, they received an adequate amount of income replacement? Could they ask for help when they needed it? Health crises revealed the pre-existing strengths and fault lines in people's relationships with money. Sometimes, their marriages just couldn't survive the effects of the health earthquake.

As a medical school professor, I've always been interested in helping doctors make it easier for patients to do the right things for their health. Over time, this interest has expanded into other domains of life, including the domain of financial well-being. It turns out that money and medicine are a lot alike in terms of the problems people have in following through with the recommendations they are given. There are systemic barriers that can get in the way – things like access to education and other resources. In both medicine and finance, professionals spend too much time talking and not enough time listening to the people they are trying to help. I wrote my book, Advice That Sticks, to help financial practitioners give advice more effectively.

Dr. Somers illuminated that *everything* touches money. She traced her money story back to her childhood, what she learned from her parents and what behaviors around finance she observed from her sibling. Then she paved her own road in the way of financial literacy and consultancy.

Next up, it's your turn to craft your money story and understand your money messages. Part I provided the background for you to better understand how deeply rooted money is in your DNA, and how important it is for you to tell your money stories. We hope that you are excited to start your journey, to live and reveal your *Courageous Money* movie and share it with others!

In Part II, you will learn many ways to talk about money in a fun, enlightening and revealing ways that have everything to do with learning, growing, teaching, stretching and expanding your mind, and not amounts. Here, you can change the way you talk about money, one story at a time.

# PART II. WELCOME TO YOUR ACTION-ADVENTURE MOVIE

*"Wherever you go, go with all your heart." ~Confucius*

# Your Action-Adventure Movie in Money National Park

It's time to begin creating your action-adventure movie on-location in Money National Park. You will be equal parts explorer, adventurer, writer, actor, director, observer and audience!

Because money is such a serious topic and one that isn't easy to talk about, our goal is to make navigating money talk a little more fun and relatable. On your journey you will stop at adventure sites to explore and create your movie, scene by scene. With Money National Park as your backdrop, you will have money conversations and tell your stories from each adventure scene; each scene being a clip of your *Courageous Money* movie. Your action-adventure movie is all about understanding and insight, reflection and possibilities, which ultimately leads to choices and happy trails. It will reveal your relationship with money and the influence it has in your life. Basically, your *Courageous Money* movie will change the way you talk about money...one story at a time.

# What is Money National Park?

Some of our best moments in life have been spent exploring national parks all over the world. The wonder, awe and learning they provide is often a once-in-a-lifetime experience. Our goal is to create the backdrop for you, with money as your plot.

While our approach is unique, we encourage anyone who is more literal in their thinking to give it a chance!

At Money National Park, each of the adventure sites are associated with money message sources—in other words, where your money messages came from; upbringing, culture, gender, generation, and temperament. It also covers real-life scenarios such as career choices, first job, first big purchase, relationships and tragedy. The best part about this park is that like real national parks, it is very versatile and there's something for everyone! Your adventure can be a trip you take solo, as a couple, with a book club, friends or as a family. Personally, we like the more-the-merrier approach so you may even meet a few new acquaintances along the way who are traveling on a parallel journey. Road Trip!

You can document your journey the old-fashioned way (journaling), by virtual means (video, photos, on social media), in-person with verbal storytelling to anyone who will listen, and even by Zoom! Visit MoneyNationalPark.com to find additional resources. *Courageous Money* concepts and story sparks can be used at the dinner table, holiday gatherings or on your next vacation. Whatever means you choose to document your money movie adventure, we highly encourage you to share your *Courageous Money* experiences with others and us on social media by tagging us @MoneyNationalPark and #CourageousMoney.

In the end, the most important gift, both given and received, will be the ability to talk more easily about money and share money stories with one another. One word of caution, there may be different perspectives of the same scene from your chosen fellow travelers, based on who is telling the story. What you view or recall from your perspective may not even be recognizable as the same scene from another person's perspective; recall the various movie theatres mentioned by Don Miguel-Ruiz. This is not about being right, it is about telling your money stories from your perspective and encouraging others to do the same. Be open to hearing new perspectives and seeing new angles regarding the same event. In the end, the culmination of stories that you shared on your adventure through Money National Park is *your* movie. You're simply sharing them one story at a time. And, although you will be sharing stories from all the adventure scenes, when you reach the end of the trail, your movie will play on. Memorable moments will continue to create additional scenes, maybe enough for a sequel, or a docu-drama of your life.

# Money National Park Self-Guided Tour

This self-guided tour through Money National Park consists of three steps at each site:

## Step 1. Setting the Scene

National parks are some of the most photographed and memorable places in the world. At each adventure site (movie scene), you will be presented with content to shift your mind into that line of thinking. Allow yourself to go back to the scenes where your stories happened. Use this mental recall to tell your story; visualize the scene: where you were, who was involved, the emotions that you felt, and thoughts that you recall about that moment in your life. Allow yourself a trip down memory lane and share some of the details of your movie scene – from your perspective and encourage others to do the same

## Step 2. Story Sparks

The ultimate goal of this adventure is to find ways to talk about money and money messages in fun, non-threatening ways. The easiest way to do this is to share stories using *Story Sparks*. These Story Sparks are conversation starters (questions). Each site offers numerous questions. Your role will be to scan through them and identify which one(s) are the most relevant for you to answer. You can answer some or all. These questions are designed to help you think about where your money messages came from and will range from easy to very deep and reflective. Be prepared to relive these money stories and then share them with friends and family when you feel comfortable doing so. Additional tools will be available at MoneyNationalPark.com.

## Step 3. Money Messages

National parks and movies alike have been known to create magical moments that are remembered forever. Similarly, your stories from each scene may create some memorable moments. But not just any memorable moment, moments that developed your money messages. These will be lessons learned or key insights having to do with money, your relationship with money or how money has influenced your thoughts and behaviors. These are pivotal moments and elicit solid insight for you to ponder and then, if needed, adopt new beliefs.

Here, you will also have the opportunity to take a step back, think about your money messages, affirm those serving you and revise or eliminate those that are not. Many of your money messages will not change, but quite possibly, some will.

Cynthia, our finance and estate planning attorney mentioned earlier, shared one of her stories that exemplifies money messages being re-evaluated. Cynthia grew up watching her parents make every dollar count and be very practical in their purchases. She and her sister received one new pair of school shoes each year and this one pair had to last the whole school year, which meant they were not necessarily the cute or fashionable type, more like Army shoes that were embarrassing to wear. Because of this she learned to be a saver and very practical. While not a spender, she likes to give to others. To this day, she does not buy things for herself, although she enjoys being generous with others.

When Cynthia got married, her husband had different spending habits that were engrained in him from an early age. Being raised on a large farm, the family would harvest their annual crop, sell it and then buy everything they had waited for over the year in one big shopping spree (including large items such as a new car). He carried these behaviors with him into adulthood.

This combination of vastly different money behaviors and spending habits was an eye-opener in their early years of marriage. With her husband accepting a corporate job, his desire to do big shopping sprees on a regular basis did not match his routine paychecks.

As a couple, they knew that they needed to re-evaluate their money messages and find common ground. For the first few years, until they could change their spending habits, they decided to use his paycheck and a small part of hers for everyday/monthly expenses. Cynthia then deferred portions of her income until year end; at which point she would take a larger distribution as a lump sum so that they could make some larger purchases together. Over the years, they both settled into new spending habits. He now saves more than she does and loves investing, too!

# Fellow Explorers

As with every journey, you run into fellow travelers and Money National Park is no different. The explorers described here, completed their journey through Money National Park, where they created their own *Courageous Money* movie. We asked them to journey through Money National Park as a pilot group, and you will hear parts of their movies unfold at the various adventure scenes. Their individual money stories were more captivating than we could have hoped for, and convinced us that the practice of sharing money stories is powerful and useful. The explorers made recommendations that *Courageous Money* should be used beyond families, and introduced to teams and organizations. Our explorers came from many different backgrounds and circumstances. Meet your fellow explorers (in their own words) and see who you most relate to:

**Introducing your fellow explorers:**

**Carefree Candi**: "My parents did not have a bank account and only operated with cash as a lot of working-class families did in the 1980s. Even with meager earnings, they demonstrated freedom, fun and independence in spending, particularly on objects for the house. Our family only took one or two road trips a year within the same state. The annual vacation car seemed always in need of repair. In essence, my family banked on getting by and "living today like there was no tomorrow." As the founder of a successful Manhattan-based writing and editing agency, I can think of my parents as "storytellers" of financial freedom among the working class of their day. While working insanely hard to never repeat their mistakes in the 21<sup>st</sup> century, I'm an independent woman who helps people make their dreams come true and knows all too well how powerful your "story" is to life. And I say, courageously edit it often!"

**Venturous Vin**: I'm the CEO of Grand Metropolitan, an American multi-national luxury goods holding company founded in Beverly Hills, California. in 2000. The group owns over 126 brand subsidiaries that have conducted over $250 billion in revenue collectively since their founding, originating in 1787. Many of the brands have been leading employers and institutions in their local communities, raising millions of dollars over the years for a range of charities and causes. I'm ready to go on this journey with you.

**Daring Denise**: After retiring from the financial world, I'm an administrator for an Estate Planning Council. Exploring money messages has taken me to undiscovered places. I didn't realize that so many of my life events, including how I raised my kids to think about money, had something to do with the way I look at money. And this is spoken from a person that has had a successful career in the financial industry! I'm looking forward to sharing my story.

**Mega Myles**: I happened to journey through Money National Park during the week of the official global launch of my company, Superbia, a financial marketplace for the LGBTQ+ community with a mission to eradicate discrimination and accelerate equality—the first of its kind. The goal of Superbia is to become the trusted safe space for banking, life and health insurances, and money management solutions that work for Superbia Members and for our community. I am thrilled to share my money stories after four years of sheer grit, while my dream company (and impact on the world) is manifesting.

**Power-of-the-Purse Gina**: I am the quintessential stay-at-home mom and self-proclaimed Nordstrom ambassador. I love to shop and I'm good at it! I took this journey along with my parents and they shared funny stories that I had never heard before. I have a notebook filled with notes that I took. I also went on this journey with my husband. I'm eager to share these experiences with you!

**Mountaineer Matt**: "Winding my way through Money National Park has been quite a trip down memory lane. As a Charles Schwab Financial Consultant, I love helping people make sense of money and to achieve their goals in life. (Full disclosure, Matthew is the personal financial advisor of the authors; so of course, trust every word he says!)

**The Authors:** You will find our full money movies showing in Part III.

*Lights, camera, action!* Time to start your movie in Money National Park.

# Entrance Gate

Welcome to Money National Park! So glad that you finally arrived at the entrance gate! It's time to pay your entrance fee. Your fee is in the form of a question and all of your fellow explorers, including those traveling this adventure with you, must answer:

*What 3 words come to mind when you think about money?*

Take your time. When you are ready, begin documenting and sharing your adventure.

**Fellow Explorers**

Each of the fellow explorers paid their entrance fee by answering this question. Some of these words will be more fully explained as their movies are revealed.

**Carefree Candi**: Fear. Joy. Opportunity.

**Venturous Vin**: Luxury. Equity. Responsibility.

**Daring Denise**: Ruler. Lack. Fear.

**Mega Myles**: Fleeting. Renewable. Means.

**Power-of-the-Purse Gina**: Gratitude. Family. Comfort.

**Mountaineer Matt**: Freedom. Independence. Tragedy.

**Quentin Fottrell,** honorary explorer and author of the foreword: Work. Freedom. Safety

# Adventure Scene #1: Money Mindset Mine

*"Wanna see how people really are? Wait until money is involved!"* ~*Choulan Saahab*

**Step 1. Setting the Scene**

Your movie begins with a scenic stop at Money Mindset Mine. A historic site that takes you back to the beginning of your lifetime as you explore the roles you play when it comes to money, what we call your *Money Mindset*. Your money mindset is tied to both your temperament and your values. Your inherent temperament (personality traits you were born with) and your values (some inherent, some learned, and some adopted over time) shape your money mindset(s). Some people gravitate toward one money mindset more than others. Some people can relate to all four. Your money mindset is an integral driver of your behaviors and influences your communication style as it relates to money.

The four money mindsets are *Saver, Spender, Investor and Giver*. Savers and investors lean more to left-brain analytical thinking. Spenders and givers lean more to right-brain creative and non-conforming thinking. Let's explore each.

Read through the following table and note the money mindset(s) you relate to the most. The connection should feel natural, not contrived. Some people will relate to more than one money mindset, while others will relate to only one. There are no wrong choices. As you read through the characteristics, you may not relate to every single characteristic listed. That's okay! In fact, if that's the case, it gives you more to talk about with others. You may notice that you find some mindset descriptors to be aspirational in nature or maybe abhorrent; again, another conversation starter. Feel free to highlight or annotate so you can remember your thoughts later when you are sharing your experience with your fellow explorers.

| SAVER | | |
|---|---|---|
| *Words that describe the saver* | | |
| Accomplishment-driven | Loyal | Direct |
| Fair | Responsible | In-control |
| Task-oriented /checklist | Time-focused | Structured |
| *Core values that savers hold true* | | |
| Security | Loyalty | Honesty |
| Responsibility | Justice | Credentials |
| *Positive traits of savers* | | |
| Great organizers and rule makers | Able to assimilate a lot of information quickly | Takes charge of a situation that requires it |
| *Savers under stress or to the extreme* | | |
| Over-controlling | Opinionated | Not good at listening |

| SPENDER | | |
|---|---|---|
| *Words that describe the spender* | | |
| Entrepreneurial | Non-conforming | Gut-thinking |
| Visionary | Risk-taker | Fun |
| Competitive | Influential | Inventor |
| *Core values that spenders hold true* | | |
| Freedom | Ingenuity | Innovation |
| Risk | Action | Ideation |
| *Positive traits of spenders* | | |
| Makes things happen | Adapts quickly to change | Sees the future |
| *Spenders under stress or to the extreme* | | |
| Lacks empathy | Acts first, thinks later | Exaggerates |

# COURAGEOUS MONEY: YOUR ADVENTURE THROUGH MONEY NATIONAL PARK

| INVESTOR | | |
|---|---|---|
| *Words that describe the investor* | | |
| Analytical | Logical | Thinkers |
| Processors (of information) | Factual | Intelligent |
| Researchers | Stoic | Sarcastic/Dry |
| *Core values that most investors hold true* | | |
| Data | Information | Intellect |
| Respect (must be earned) | Facts | Retrospection/History |
| *Positive traits of investors* | | |
| Provides multiple scenarios for problem-solving | Research is key to good investments | Works well independently |
| *Investors under stress or to the extreme* | | |
| Analysis paralysis | Talks down to people/sarcastic | Non-communicative/in their head too much |

| GIVER | | |
| --- | --- | --- |
| *Words that describe the giver* | | |
| Empathic | Creative | Generous |
| Thoughtful | Caring | Accepting |
| Tolerant | Kind/Compassionate | Spiritual |
| *Core values that givers hold true* | | |
| Gratitude | Philanthropy/Giving | Family |
| Relationships | Grace | Sacrifice |
| *Positive traits of givers* | | |
| Have excellent intuition | Knows how to bring people together | Have huge hearts |
| *Givers under stress or to the extreme* | | |
| Passive-aggressive | Prone to overwhelm/guilt (can't say no) | Requires a lot of validation |

## Step 2. Story Sparks

Scan through the list of questions below and find ones that resonate with you. Have fun answering your selected questions, listen to others answer theirs and, in the end, everyone just might see things a little differently.

1. Which money mindset(s) most resonate with you and why?
2. How do your money habits reflect this mindset?
3. As a _____ (Saver, Spender, Investor or Giver) I enjoy...
4. The story that best exhibits me being a _____ (Saver, Spender, Investor or Giver – or any combination of them) is...
5. Your money mindset is your belief regarding what money is for, its purpose: saving, spending, investing and giving. How is this true for you?
6. If traveling with others, have each person share their money

mindset(s) and then discuss the following:

7. How you are different or the same in your thinking?
8. What values do you share?
9. Where do you find common ground in making decisions?
10. How can you see each other's traits as an asset?

## Step 3. Money Messages

Money messages can be summarized as your lesson(s) learned, key insights having to do with money, your relationship with money or how money has influenced your thoughts and behaviors. This is also where you will have the opportunity to affirm the money messages that are serving you and then identify any that are no longer serving you and revise or eliminate them. Many times, we have money messages that are no longer serving us yet we do not realize that we have the power to change or eliminate them. Being that this is the first adventure scene in Money National Park, here is an example from our Explorers to help illustrate Steps 2 and 3.

### *Fellow Explorers: Carefree Candi and Power-of-the-Purse Gina at Money Mindset Mine*

**Candi's Money Mindsets:** I am a spender and a giver. As a professional woman in my forties with my own business, I'm a frequent traveler. Money messages learned in my youth about living in the moment fueled spending in the moment. I've had to rein in both my spending and my giving. Now, I am married to a woman from Rio de Janeiro, Brazil, which makes for twice the money messages between us. In fact, she is more of the saver and investor, and brings a colorful culture of money to our dynamics. Our combined money messages didn't blend initially. They needed to be shaken from our family trees and distilled in order for us to chat about them.

*Money Message:* Work hard, play hard; it's my money so I can spend it the way I want. Would I change my money message here? As a couple, most certainly: Let's devise a new money story—one that equally blends Spender, Giver, Investor, and Saver and takes into consideration a once-in-a-lifetime pandemic so we will have a secure future and will be able to have the lifestyle we want for the long-term together.

**Gina's Money Mindset:** For the record, I'm a spender! I love to shop. I like nice things. We have two homes, each in a different state. In one location, a small town in Colorado, they don't care what brand of purse is on my arm. In Arizona, they do, so I have two very different closets. One with monogrammed designer purses, and one with a backpack and sling purse from Dakin. Over the years, we've lived in many "model homes" tied to the family construction business, which meant they had to be well decorated and always clean. I became the interior designer for the models, which fueled my love of shopping. My daughter worked at Nordstrom's in Scottsdale, so that got me in trouble, too! When I was in my thirties one of my social networks was a group of "real housewives," there was definitely a pull to "keep up with the Joneses," which led me to bad choices and exhaustion. Sometimes you have friends to teach you lessons of what not to do!

*Money Message:* Shopping is life! Would I rewrite my money message? It is hard to admit this, but I would change my money message (my motto) *from* "Shopping is life" *to* "Shopping isn't everything." When I tried to keep up with the Joneses, I got in trouble and now I treat credit differently. I'm instilling this in my kids: Don't buy anything if you can't pay for it. Pay off the balance every month, and take a moment to evaluate 'why' you're buying that item—for you or for other's perception of you?

# Adventure Scene #2: Fountain of Youth

Fountain of Youth

*"There is a fountain of youth: it is your mind, your talents, the creativity you bring to your life and the lives of people you love. When you learn to tap this source, you will truly have defeated age." ~Sophia Loren*

**Step 1. Setting the Scene**

The Fountain of Youth scene is all about money messages that you learned while growing up; from your parents, relatives, influential people, whoever was in your circle of friends or your parent's circle of friends, the stability of your household, and even your zip code (the location you grew up in and your socio-economic status). *Culture, gender, generation and sibling influences will not be covered here, as they each provide enough Oscar-winning content to create their own scenes in Money National Park.* Fountain of Youth covers stories from the following areas of your life:

1. Your zip code and/or country that you grew up in
2. Family vacations
3. Schooling
4. Family transportation
5. Household finances: How money flowed to and through the house
6. Household configuration (two parents, one parent, divorced, blended)
7. Emotions associated with money, such as abundance or scarcity
8. Gift giving

These Fountain of Youth early money messages from your upbringing play a massive role in influencing you as an adult. For now, *think about stories having to do with your earliest memories of when and how you learned the value of money.*

In developing your movie script, there will be many stories that emerge at this location. That's okay, you can have multiple stories in one scene (think flashbacks as part of your movie with lots of little vignettes).

Let your mind wander and land on these flashbacks to develop the scene. Everyone has a story to share about their household configuration and how money played its part. In families, individuals see these things differently, so while you may be convinced it was one way, others may have perceived the same event differently. Be curious about their perspectives of stories and allow everyone their truth.

**Step 2. Story Sparks**

Have fun answering selected questions throughout this adventure. These memories will spark stories, which is the point.

**Zip code**

The location or area(s) that you grew up in, including your home country and any evidence about your socio-economic status

1. What is your story regarding where you lived or grew up?
2. Could you tell if your family was living differently than other families

(wealthier or poorer)?

3.  How about your extended family, did any of them live different lifestyles than yours and if so, did that matter to you?
4.  At what age did you realize there were inequities in how you or other people lived?
5.  If you lived in a different country, for instance, what differences did that provide in terms of learned money messages?

## Family vacations (or lack thereof)

1.  Share stories or overall themes about where you went on vacation, where you stayed, how you traveled, who paid for what and who planned the outings.
2.  When you traveled were your trips expensive or modest?
3.  If you couldn't afford to go on vacation, what did you do instead? how did that impact you?
4.  What did you learn from your vacation experiences?
5.  What money messages were conveyed as part of your vacation experiences?
6.  What money messages were conveyed if you didn't take vacations?
7.  What vacation habits or traditions did you carry with you?

## Schooling

Schools that you attended play a large role in forming early money messages.

1.  Did you attend public or private school?
2.  Did you have money to participate in extracurricular activities (sports, clubs, bands, etc.)? Maybe your school didn't charge for extracurricular activities.
3.  In school, did you ever feel like you had "more than" or "less than?" At what age did you notice this discrepancy?
4.  What expectations were set at home or school about attending college?
5.  Was anything communicated or assumed about who would pay for

it?

6. How was your college, related activities and expenses paid for (parents, scholarships, financial aid, you working, etc.)?
7. If few or none of your extended family went to college, what is the primary reason? If you were the first to go to college, what motivated you?

## Family transportation

Family cars, or in many cases, *the* family car, makes a great story in your movie. Your first car will be discussed at the Park Gift Shop scene.

1. What is your family car story and what money messages were conveyed?
2. What kind of car(s) did you grow up with (limo/chauffer, newer, older, nicer, basic, luxury, classic in a good way, classic in a bad way, good ole rusty)?
3. How many cars were available to the household?
4. Were they owned or leased?
5. How often did your family change cars?
6. How were/are cars associated (or not) with status in your family?
7. Are cars a status symbol for you?

## Household Finances: Money flowing to and through the house

1. While growing up, what did you see regarding how money came into and out of the house?
2. What was it spent on the most (bills and basic needs, savings, giving)?
3. Was there enough to cover the monthly bills?
4. Did your family live on a budget?
5. How fast was money spent?
6. What financial accounts did you know about: Bank accounts, checking, savings, retirement or a cash stash in the house somewhere?
7. Who managed the family money/financials?

8. What do you recall about the use of credit cards?
9. Who made major purchase decisions? Were you involved in any way?
10. When did someone encourage you to start saving?
11. How was money used as a reward?

## Household configuration

1. What story would you tell about your household configuration: Traditional family with the male as breadwinner and female as homemaker? Did both parents work? Were you raised by a single parent, divorced parents, adoptive parent(s), non-traditional parent(s)?
2. Any noticeable gender income/pay inequities between parents'?
3. If you had divorced parents, were there inequities in lifestyles between the households? Did you watch one parent struggle while the other prospered? Any memories about child support being paid or not? How about growing up in a household where your parents stayed together or a divorce was delayed/avoided solely for money reasons?
4. Were you part of a blended family? Possibly a blended family that came together from different cultures or socio-economic levels?
5. What was your parents' view of money: What do you believe to be their money mindsets (Saver, Spender, Investor, Giver)? Which parent(s) are you more like and why?

## Emotions and money: feelings of abundance or scarcity

Money messages rooted in childhood emotions tied to abundance or scarcity run deep within us. Formulate your stories here by considering the following questions:

1. What emotions were associated with money within the family—Positive, strained, angry, scarcity, entitlement, etc.?
2. Were there arguments because of money? How did they affect you?
3. Was money readily available or were you surviving month to month?

4. What was your overall feeling about your financial security back then?
5. What residual effects do you have from these experiences?
6. What was considered expensive to you as a kid?
7. Did you go to work at a young age to help out?
8. From your perspective, which did you perceive to be more important: family or money?

## Gifts, giving and holiday spending

Now, layer on how gifts, giving and holiday spending adds to your movie.

1. When you were young, when and where did you see people giving (tithing, philanthropy, charity, helping friends or family, etc.)? Were you ever aware of how much was being given or why?
2. What was the first gift that you remember giving (monetary and/or non-monetary)?
3. How does gift giving make you feel?
4. What is your opinion of gift giving today?
5. What kinds of gifts do you give today?
6. What is the most meaningful gift that you have ever given (monetary and/or non-monetary)?
7. What is the most meaningful gift that you have ever received (monetary or non-monetary)?
8. Consider holidays and other occasions for gift giving and receiving: Describe some typical gifts that you received while growing up. Which were your favorites? Why? Was there enough? What gifts did you typically give?
9. Did any family member try to equalize gifting, either by counting the number of gifts or mentally tabulating the overall monetary value?
10. What role did your grandparents or extended family play in gift giving?
11. Did gifts have any hidden meanings or were they used as leverage?

## Step 3. Money Messages

# COURAGEOUS MONEY: YOUR ADVENTURE THROUGH MONEY NATIONAL PARK

Document and share your adventure. Summarize your money messages and key insights from your formative years' movie scenes; remember to affirm, revise or eliminate these money messages accordingly.

### *Fellow Explorer: Daring Denise at the Fountain of Youth*

There was always lack. My parents always worked three or four jobs. It was drilled in us that if they didn't work so hard, we wouldn't have food or the necessities for life. As a child, you're grasping lack or abundance from what your parents are talking about and how they are behaving. My circumstances were unconventional. I grew up in the suburbs of Buffalo, New York. That's where the jobs were. There were five kids. My father got a job at Pepsi Co. driving a truck and his boss hired my mother as their maid to help with their children. She also had a job at a psychiatric center to take care of mentally challenged children.

Black people could not buy houses in certain neighborhoods, but occasionally a boss would buy a house for the family, ours did that for us. We lived in a nice house in the suburbs of New York, but we didn't have food in the fridge and furniture was sparse. We went to a nice school, but we didn't have the right clothes or school supplies. In elementary school, we were the only black kids. That came with issues of their own. I loved math and reading. School was a haven to shut out the noise of other things going on.

As a teen, my pen circled a job opening for a bank teller [in the newspaper -that's what job seekers did back then] I didn't know anything about banking. I didn't know about checking or savings accounts. I got the job and my colleagues taught me every aspect about banking. Most importantly, and what broke a cycle for me, I learned that when people got paid and they didn't just cash their paychecks—They deposited the money! They didn't necessarily need to use all of the money right away. The more deposit slips that I filled out week to week, the more their money added up, protected in an account. This was revolutionary to me! I came home to tell my husband and we started to deposit our checks in savings, checking and investment accounts. Our money grew... This was life altering for us.

But my childhood anxieties around money were still there. I operated on the fear that I wouldn't have enough money to pay bills all my life, and I didn't realize how much I was transferring it to my kids. As soon as my kids turned 16 years old, I made them get a job. I taught them a portion of their paychecks should be deposited and the rest was for them to enjoy life. By the time they left home, they all had decent savings. All three of my children have college educations. No one taught me finances as a young person, I had to learn as I went along. In turn, I made sure my kids learned basic finance knowledge along the way.

*Money Message:* Know that you have more power than you think. You might not have the right words or messages, but don't be silenced. Wisdom will teach you whatever fear others instill in you are not true. Wisdom will also tell you that all that stuff you're striving to purchase is not as important as your daily living and relationships. Money is really important, but we can't let it have so much control. I may have been more relaxed had I not put so much fight into achieving financial stability. Working hard is noble and rewarded, but be smart! Being smart allows you to balance work with play. Playing hard is important, too.

# Adventure Scene #3: Gender Mountain

*"First they ignore you, then they laugh at you, then they fight you, then you win."*
*~Mahatma Gandhi*

### Step 1. Setting the Scene

Like it or not, gender roles still play a very large part in our money messaging worldwide, and if you are gender non-binary, there are even greater nuances.

The gender pay gap still exists. And although it is narrowing ever so gradually—with a predicted 100 years more to eliminate it, white women in the U.S. still make only 80 cents on the dollar compared to their male counterparts. Black women and Hispanic women experience even greater pay disparity, 64 cents and 55 cents respectively. Women still working over age 65 earn 67 cents on the dollar and here is the tell-all about gender: transgender women (male-to-female) make 30% less after they transition and transgender men (female-to-male) actually earned more after their transition. Yet, strikingly, about half of all transgender individuals earn $15,000 or less per year and only 37% are employed full-time.

*The Moment of Lift*, by Melinda Gates, mentioned previously, is part memoir and part call to action for moving society forward by empowering women. Melinda states:

> If the barrier is distance, money, knowledge, or stigma, we have to offer tools and information that are closer, cheaper and less tainted by stigma. To fight poverty, we have to see and study the barriers and figure out if they're cultural, or social, or economic, or geographic, or political, and then go around or through them so the poor aren't cut off from benefits others enjoy... As soon as we began to spend more time understanding how people live their lives, we saw that so many of the barriers to advancement—and so many of the causes of isolation—can be traced to the limits put on the lives on women... If you want to lift up humanity, empower women. It's the most comprehensive, pervasive, high-leverage investment you can make in human beings.

Awareness, education and self-confidence are key factors in making a difference. Start commanding your power with more financially related tasks, knowledge and skills. Helpful hints on how to do this were provided in Part I, specifically the sections on Finding your Courage in Finance and Money Confidence.

In addition to pay inequalities, there are other powers at play at Gender Mountain. In relationships, there are often inequities in both power and pay. Over time, each person will 'seek to own or control something' to find balance within a relationship. This is how individuals maintain their sense of self-worth and balance being part of a whole. Typically, whoever is the primary breadwinner has more perceived power; a financial power that holds clout. This is why some men have a hard time when women make more money than they do. Also known as *fiscal inequality* or *financial diversity*, our archetypes tell us that this is not the norm and that men are supposed to be the breadwinners and the rulers of the roost. We all know that this is not the case anymore, but history and programming are hard to recapitulate. But it is reassuring to know that we are moving in a direction where men are more comfortable with this scenario and credit is now given to men who can accept the secondary breadwinner role, or supportive role, with grace and kindness!

This natural controlling instinct comes from our desire to be good at something and a need to control that is deep within us. Have you ever noticed that when one area of your world is out of control, you will over-control other areas, such as if work is out of control, you will become more controlling at home or if home seems out of control, you will exert more control at work so that you can 'feel in control' of something?

In a relationship, one person may have the financial power on their side while the other person navigates accordingly to balance it by finding other things to control: the kids, family, kitchen, household, gardening, laundry, lawncare, cyber world/technology in the home, etc. Control in some of these cases may look more like project management.

What does all of this have to do with gender messages and money? Historically speaking, women have gained or balanced their relationship power by taking on many of the non-financial duties. While one could argue plenty of women wish to embrace these roles (and that is okay), many feel stuck in them. And this feeling of being stuck is also a great source of stress for many.

On the "Index Fund Advisors" show, with Robin Powell, finance journalist, Dr. Somers said that women tend to stress about money more than men—to the point that they're losing sleep. "Sometimes that's because they don't have sufficient knowledge of their own family finances. They're not the ones in control. ...You know how when you're the passenger in a car and you are glad somebody else is driving, but then you realize that you have absolutely no control of the car if needed? It's that kind of stress."

Before we move into your gender movie scene, you may find this next piece of knowledge fascinating. Besides inequities in power and pay, another source of gender inequity comes from how media, manufacturers and marketing all perpetuate gender discrepancies that result in biased money messages from an early age. So obvious and right under our noses, are the inequities in how little boys and girls are raised—from expected career and education choices to the fabric that is manufactured for each. For decades, boys are steered toward higher income-earning degrees and careers, as in doctor, lawyer, and STEM jobs (science, technology, engineering and math); and despite STEM's best efforts to attract girls, girls are still steered more toward less lucrative helping professions, e.g., nurse, teacher. Although there are a higher percentage of bachelor's degrees being awarded to females than males (58 vs. 42 percent), in STEM fields, a lower percentage of bachelor's degrees were awarded to females than to males (21 vs. 79 percent).

Regarding clothing inequities, did you know that little girls' clothing is intentionally made of thinner, more flimsy materials, representing a more delicate, softer, fragile-natured child that is encouraged to partake in more subdued and cautious activities so they don't ruin their clothes? Also colored pink, with tighter sleeves, a plunging neckline, ruffled or scalloped ribbon edges, and cinched at the waist so they can be associated with being a princess—still assumed to be taken care of by a prince? While little boys' clothing is made of thicker, sturdier, longer wearing materials, often dark colors, square and boxy with loose sleeves that allow for plenty of movement, with 'Super Something' printed on it, all representing a tougher, more resilient, more durable, 'super' person. These differences in clothing turn into adult nuances that support cultural expectations: a man's suit means they are more serious and practical and a woman's flouncy dress means they are more frivolous and superficial.

Many fashion designers are now on board to create more gender-neutral clothing. Starting in 2015, Target made a pledge to move away from gender-based signs and make a big push to equalize these fashion differences between genders. Go Target!

Gender differences such as these get imprinted as very early money messages and can be extremely difficult, if not impossible, to change. Unfortunately, these systemic issues are bigger than any one of us, but we are moving in the right direction and it has to start somewhere. Own what *you* can!

## Step 2. Story Sparks

### Power balance

1. How is your family traditional or non-traditional when it comes to stereotypical gender norms?
2. When growing up, was there an equal balance between men/women (or partners) in the financial roles and responsibilities within your house?
3. Who controlled what domains: raising the kids, cooking, general household duties, lawncare, grocery shopping, gardening, electronics, computers, home/car maintenance, spending, money earning and money management?
4. How are these balanced in your household now? If not balanced, why?

### A woman's path

1. You may recall from Part I that 80% of women will outlive their male counterpart. What observations do you have about how women in your family became/will become more involved with their finances?
2. By choice, death, divorce, illness, other or never - what is your path to knowing how to manage your money/finances? What do you want it to be?
3. What do you need to do, know more about, find out or explore in order to be more financially confident and capable?
4. What (if anything) do you need from others (family, lawmakers, employers) in order to improve your financial outcomes?

### If you are gender non-binary

1. How has gender-identity affected your career, earnings, finances or relationship with money?
2. What is your money story? What do you want it to be?
3. What do you need to do, know more about, find out or explore in order to be financially confident and capable?

4. What (if anything) do you need from others (family, lawmakers, employers) in order to improve your financial outcomes?

## Career biases

1. Did you witness or experience any discrepancies (inside and outside the house) in what boys were told versus girls regarding school, life and career choices?
2. Were there any expectations, implied or explicit, around your career choice or working habits based on your gender (i.e., messages such as: get a good, stable job and stay with it for years, vs. do what you love even if there's no money in that career; or, make sure you make enough to provide for a family)?
3. Were you influenced by stereotypical gender specific roles or career choices (boy = doctors or lawyers and girl = teachers and nurses) or were you one to break the mold (male secretary or female neurosurgeon)? Please note, if this applies to you, it's a great thing and the world is a better place because of your choices! Just realize that many paths have been influenced by historical gender biases in addition to a person's natural desires.
4. What language do you use with your kids/grandkids and is it gender neutral regarding careers, schooling, activities, groups, clubs, toys etc.?

## Gender norms and stereotypes

1. Gender norms and stereotypes are embedded in our culture and still drive our everyday lives and socialization to a great degree. What is one thing that you can do or have done to break out of gender norms and lead the way for others to do the same – especially relating to money? What is the benefit in doing so? (Consider how gender norms may be affecting your kids or grandkids for instance.)
2. If you had the courage to do more in this space, what would it look like for you? What education, help or support would you need or be willing to provide to someone else to make this happen?

3. If you are a manager of people, are your male/female employees paid equally? What is your role in closing the gender gap?

**Step 3. Money Messages**

Document and share your adventure. Summarize your money messages and key insights from your Gender Mountain movie scene(s); remember to affirm, revise or eliminate these money messages accordingly.

### *Fellow Explorer: Mega Myles at Gender Mountain*

I got married to a wonderful woman and had three kids. We bought a house outside of Toronto; everyone had a white-picket fence, drove the same vehicles, went to the tennis club, and went on holiday somewhere in the Caribbean every year. The pressure to earn and keep all these balls in the air was tremendous. We would lie in bed and think, how are we going to pay for this house? We made it, keeping up with the Joneses for seventeen years until we got divorced. Everyone cautioned me against divorce because starting over would be a nightmare. We realized that after seventeen years, our marriage had come to an end, and not just because I since understood my authentic self to be a gay man. We separated to enter our own new season of life. At the time, my wife made four times more money than me. Lawyers and friends who had been through divorces were on top of this, urging me to make certain demands of her, but I refused.

This was when I put money in its place. I realized that starting over financially, which took me a decade, was meaningless compared to the value of living happy. Money will never outrank a relationship for me. It will never be placed above the people I love and the work I do for Superbia. The moment I distinguished this, the problem I had with money vanished. And surprising things have happened for me such as when I received an unexpected $24,000 check in the mail – just when things were tough. And today my ex-wife is my best friend.

*Money Message:* Knowing what I know today, I may have started Superbia for the LGBTQ+ population sooner! Superbia is a systemic shock to the financial services system. The model of Superbia can be applied to marginalized communities in countries of similar market drivers around the world. Organizing the community differently creates new powers in choosing for itself, and in the ability to sustainably care for itself. We have a sustained mechanism built into Superbia that will return hundreds of millions of dollars to the community in a relatively short time. The more Superbia is used by the community, the more it returns to the community. There are financial benefits that are triumphant. We can take these lessons of how money fits inside human decency; it is an incredibly important aspect of living in a modern world. We are looking at about 16 million people who have been systematically denied the same access to awareness, education, approval, and just the ability to listen and learn about money.

My key insight, money is essential and has a priority. Money's worth is in the freedom of time it gives you to be with those you want to be with and do what you want to do. People are fundamentally progressive and social animals. Money allows you to exercise those muscles rather than just accumulate goods or savings in your bank account.

# Adventure Scene #4: Generation Trail

*"Messages about money are passed down from generation to generation, worn and chipped like the family dishes." ~Suze Orman*

## Step 1. Setting the Scene

What money messages were prevalent during your generation?

### Silent Generation/Traditionalists (born 1927-1946)

In the Silent/Traditionalist generation, men made up the bulk of the breadwinners, and women made up the bulk of the bread bakers—except for during WWII when women proved they could do "men's work" and took on the bulk of manufacturing jobs producing war materials—of course after the war was over, they were dismissed without ceremony. Most commonly known as "children of the Depression," the silent generation brought the strong work ethic of their parents into the factories of industrialized society. They grew up during lean times, including the Great Depression and World War II. This generation sacrificed greatly for their country by volunteering in great numbers for military service at the expense of personal financial gain. Often leaving their young families to persevere alone in favor of the "greater good." They consider work and service a privilege and their strong work ethic paid off a they are considered the wealthiest generation. Loyalty, thriftiness, and conformity characterize this generation.

## Baby Boomers (born 1946-1964)

This generation grew up during the Civil Rights Movement and the Cold War. They created the term "workaholic" and are the largest generation and workforce to date; putting their work life first and living the true "American Dream," which encompassed kids, a 9-to-5 career, a house, and a minivan. Two income households were born in this generation meaning double the earning and spending power. Boomers had pivotal roles in societal milestones and lived through major historic events, such as the assassinations of JFK, Robert Kennedy, and Martin Luther King, Jr., the walk on the Moon, Vietnam War, women's rights movement, the Stonewall Riots commencing the LGBTQ+ equal rights movement, in addition to Watergate that led to President Nixon's resignation. Because of the energy crisis, inflation and economic instability, Boomers experienced some of the hardest time finding work, similar to that experienced by Gen Z today.

## Generation X (born 1965-1980)

Gen X often gets a bad rap, being dubbed the "forgotten generation." Maybe it's because Gen X was the start of the Latch-key kids—Kids who had two parents working and had to fend for themselves after school—This was long before after-school care existed. They also had less family and financial security growing up, especially if their parents were divorced, which was also more common than in previous generations. Because of this, Gen Xers are very self-reliant and entrepreneurial. Gen X is credited with defining American pop culture; take the Walkman for example.

Being collaborative workers with little need for hierarchy, they created the "fun workspace," and began the work hard, play harder movement. Gen Xers are more direct and can generally accept defeat graciously—keeping in mind back then, everyone did not get a trophy; they learned to earn their place in the world. They have a comfortable relationship with tech; while not born with computers and internet, they were the first to have home computers and Atari! Major life events defining Gen X are the economic recession in the 80s, the stock market crash of 1987, HIV/Aids, MTV and the Challenger Disaster.

Worthy of noting in this time period is a key step in women's financial freedom; the Equal Credit Opportunity Act of 1974 allowed women to obtain credit cards separate from their husbands. Women could apply for credit without needing a co-signature from her husband or family member (father). The law made it illegal to discriminate against race, color, religion, sex and national origin. By having access to credit, the process of home buying became easier for women.

### Generation Y / Millennials (born 1981-1996)

This population grew up with a seemingly endless stream of technology advancements and communication devices. They have high levels of student debt, due to the fact that more of them have a college degree than any other generation. This generation began a trend of high competition for college admission. They are also the most ethnically and racially diverse generation. They are considered to be more optimistic, entrepreneurial, more tolerant and accepting of change, achievement-oriented, and financially savvy; working to live, rather than living to work. Major themes defining Millennials include the Oklahoma City bombing, the fall of the Berlin Wall, rise of the Internet, the O.J. Simpson murder trial, the death of Princess Diana (1997), and Y2K. These individuals are known to search for jobs that provide personal fulfillment and often higher starting pay.

Another step toward women's financial freedom occurred in 1988; the Women's Business Ownership Act allowed women to get a business loan without a male co-signer. As of December 2020, the U.S. has 12.3 million women-owned businesses that generate over $1.8 trillion a year; and in 2020 64% of new women-owned businesses were started by women of color.

## Generation Z / Digital Natives (born after 1997-2012)

Also known as the "Internet Generation," "iGen" or "Zoomers." Born into a connected world, they have grown up with all things technology: Internet from social media to invisible money (cash apps). With technology advances, such as on-line learning and a changing society, women have surpassed the number of male college graduates and are taking the lead in enhancing their financial skills and knowledge. Their entry into schools and the workforce is marked with significant competition and for many a rocky launch to independence. They are defined by instant gratification, small bits of information (texting), acceleration and innovation, and they are charged with solving the worst environmental, social, political, and economic problems in history.

### Step 2. Story Sparks

1. Which generation are you are part of?
2. Which of your generation characteristics resonate with you?
3. What money behaviors are associated with your generation?
4. What stories about money from your grandparents or great grandparents stuck with you? How different are your money messages from theirs?
5. Has anyone from a different generation influenced your habits related to money? How so?
6. What life defining events from your generation affected your money behaviors?

### Step 3. Money Messages

Document and share your adventure. Summarize your money messages and key insights from your Generation Trail movie scene(s); remember to affirm, revise or eliminate these money messages accordingly.

*Fellow Explorers: Power-of-the-Purse Gina and Venturous Vin at Generation Trail*

# COURAGEOUS MONEY: YOUR ADVENTURE THROUGH MONEY NATIONAL PARK

**Power-of-the-Purse Gina**: My parents gave me $20 a week as an allowance for chores. I had to budget that money for school lunches and things that I wanted to do on the weekend. In the summer though, we would visit my grandparents in Illinois. They would fill a coin jar every year and give it to me when we visited. Even the smallest amount would accumulate. It was fun to go and exchange the coin for dollars!

While I was visiting, grandma always pulled out blitz, a card game you played for seventy-five cents. The more we played the more I realized that those cents would add up; and if you were out of money, well then you couldn't play. Their message was that if you didn't have the money, you had nothing to spend. Similar to life, if you don't have the money, you're not allowed to spend. I learned that a little saved along the way makes a big difference in the end.

Nothing conveyed this message more than what we learned after my grandparents passed away. Here's their story: My grandparents bought a house for $1,000 that nobody would buy because the former family that lived there had smallpox. They lived there for sixty years! My dad, his sisters and parents shared one bathroom – they had to make things work.

I watched them hide money in canisters. They didn't use banks. All money was in the form of stashed cash, yet they barely spent any of it. By the time my grandparents passed away, my they had amassed millions of dollars and nobody knew it.

*Money Message:* I finally involved myself in our finances. My husband needed to take over the family construction business, which forced me to take care of the home finances. I asked a lot of questions and I still have more. I actually care about finance now and remember some of the money lessons from my grandparents. I joke that "responsibility" is not my favorite word, but "gratitude" is one of my favorites!

**Venturous Vin's Generation Trail:** I'm a Gen Xer and my parents were of the traditional generation. Both parents played distinct roles in helping with our finances. My father worked very hard to provide a good and stable lifestyle for us all. My mother worked even harder to make sure every dollar he earned gave us far greater value. She was the master of the weekly circulars that published the latest and best deals for local retailers. Even if we had already made the purchase, she would promptly load us up in the car, rushing to the merchant to demand the lower advertised price or return the item if her demands we not swiftly and politely met. If returned, she would then revisit that locale and repurchase the item at the lower price. To this day, I find myself not buying Philadelphia cream cheese unless it's on sale.

My mother was also great at volume purchasing. Once a year or so, we would go to the local grocer called *Great Scott!* She would corner the shopping cart with my little brother, Keith, sitting in the basket, leaving me as sentry until her return. She would disappear behind dented steel doors with the butcher only to reappear moments later with him in tow, hoisting a case of Tropicana orange juice frozen from concentrate over his shoulder. This sweet nectar would be served with our morning breakfasts for as much as a year, one shot glass serving at a time – no more. When requesting a second glass it was always met with a dismissive, "Have milk instead." And those PVC tubes that held the concentrate would pyramid across our kitchen counter to eventually double as drinking glasses.

*Money Message:* I remember being toted around that grocery store with my mother. Like any child I would ask constantly for things. Her reply was "I don't have any money for that," to which I would respond, "Just write a check!" This seemed to be a repeat performance at various McDonalds, Dunkin Donuts, and Rexall Pharmacies. As an adult, I appreciate my mother's teaching of saving pennies, saying no and everything has a purpose.

# Adventure Scene #5: Culture Crater

Culture Crater

*"Culture opens our hearts to one another. And the currency in culture is not money, but trust."* ~ Yo-Yo Ma

**Step 1. Setting the Scene**

Money creates its own language within every culture and subculture. Think about the various cultural attitudes, values and norms associated with money across the globe. Then, take a look at your personal networks and social circles and consider the various attitudes, values and norms associated with money. The jockeying, positioning, and posturing of money is there, even if never discussed; right down to who pays the check.

Culture refers to the attitudes, social patterns, values, beliefs and norms shared by a specific group of people. Culture Crater is the adventure that explores your native roots, social influencers, and other external elements that have helped define your beliefs about money. Every culture has different ways of viewing personal finances and 'rules' around how money is portrayed from one family to the next.

Each household is a melting pot of cultures, traditions, values and assumptions about money. Consider the following cultural assumptions:

- "Money can buy happiness." The more money I have the happier I will be: assuming that the rich have nothing to worry or complain about and that if I were rich my problems would go away.
- If I marry wealthy, I will be taken care of or don't have to worry about anything—except, maybe a relationship based on love. Is the money trade-off worth it? Listen to Moira's mother's lesson, "A man is not a plan!"
- Everything that I do in life must have a monetary value associated with it to quantify its value. For example: if I chose the arts or social services as a career, it is assumed that these careers have less earning potential and so they are seen as less desirable. If there's no money in it, what value does it have? Or, if you can't make money at it, why do it? Did you make a career choice based on earning potential?
- A good education is the key to success.
- Time is money!

**Step 2. Story Sparks**

1. Think of a community, group or network that you are a part of (neighborhood, religious, family, friends, sport, corporation, work, team, etc.). Describe the attitudes, values and norms associated with one of these groups. What spoken or non-spoken money expectations or assumptions exist within the group?
2. What cultural money messages were placed upon you through rituals, norms, religion, traditions, heritage, community, or ethnicity? What money expectations are associated with them? Think birthdays, weddings, graduation traditions, age ceremonies (bah/bar mitzvah, quinceañera), bachelor/bachelorette parties, church, giving expectations, marriage, heritage and/or ethnicity expectations.

3. What cultural traditions or assumptions influence how family is cared for, such as who takes care of aging parents or unwell family members? What is the level of obligation or expectation? How does money surface as part of these traditions or assumptions?

4. What other family situations or obligations arise that are cultural or community in nature that have a money connection, and how do you respond to these?

5. At work, what projects have you been a part of that focused on building relationships or enhancing people's skills but senior leaders only wanted to see the monetary return on investment or how much money could be made from the initiative vs the non-monetary value?

6. Money as an intangible object: We are past the Industrial and Agricultural Ages and are now moving into the Intangible Age. This new paradigm shift is already having major impacts on how companies operate. To understand the Intangible Age, think Uber and Lyft, car services that don't own cars and, in some cases, driverless, or Airbnb and Home Away, lodging and accommodation services with no hotel ownership. Money is the same way and will likely become more intangible. Think bitcoin, Apple Pay, Venmo or Zellé, electronic payments without the use of a tangible object such as a credit card or checkbook. What is your comfort level with this Intangible Age? How does it impact you or your household?

7. Most people only have a basic understanding of how money flows to and through the house and yet, our survival is dependent on it. What is your level of understanding how your money flows to and through your current household? What are you doing to help yourself and/or others in the household make sense of it?

8. It's been said that we consume money similar to how we consume food; how do your food consumption habits reflect how you consume money? (Do you devour it or savor every bite?)

**Step 3. Money Messages**

Document and share your adventure. Summarize your money messages and key insights from your Culture Crater movie scene(s); remember to affirm, revise or eliminate these money messages accordingly.

### *Fellow Explorer: Mega Myles at Culture Crater*

My parents in Canada moved far north from a small city in Saskatchewan to a village of 52 people called Silver Park and purchased the general store and gas park. As a kid, my job was to work in the general store and pump gas. My relationship with money started there when I was about six or seven years old. I had to learn the skill of making change! We had a lot of Americans tourists, hunters and fishermen who came through the village. Later, as the economy changed and tech expanded, big-box stores sprang up. Eventually the store was gone but my parents held other jobs and they were very industrious.

My first corporate job was at the Royal Bank of Canada as a teller in Toronto. I progressed to being a controller in foreign exchange. I could tell you every currency in the world and what they were worth in other countries. I had grown up with my parents watching every penny, but we bought our annual school clothes in the city, which was viewed as a privilege. Money was scarce then. But when I worked at Royal Bank, handling tens of thousands of dollars in cash at any given time, I learned that money was not scarce – it was everywhere. For fun, we would pick up gold bars to marvel at their weight, and I quickly lost sense of the worth of money... Over time I confirmed that if I combined my hard work ethics learned at an early age with my realization that money was not scarce, money would become available for me to make and spend.

*Money Message:* Understand currency and how it flows in the world. When you have a global perspective on how people live with wealth, abundance and poverty as it is defined in that country or culture, you can maintain humbleness and gratitude, no matter what you have on any given day. These days, amidst a pandemic, breath is currency.

# Adventure Scene #6: Wildlife Viewing Area

*Sibling Dynamics and Birth Order*

*"Comparison is a death knell to sibling harmony." ~Elizabeth Fishel*

**Step 1. Setting the Scene**

Your Wildlife Viewing adventure includes two different movie scenes: 1) sibling dynamics, and 2) birth order.

## Sibling Dynamics

All bets are off when it comes to sibling rivalry and the roles we play in our families. As an adult, do you ever notice that when you get together with family members everyone sort of assumes the role they were in as kids? Some people expect things to be the same. It's comfortable. Yet others keep expecting it to change, but it doesn't. Other times you may want to change the rules of the game to see if you can achieve a better outcome, which is hard work because everyone else has to want that also. Money messages are the same way; some never change, some we hope will change and others we want to change by changing the rules of the game.

Starting with sibling dynamics you will have a chance to compare your sibling relationships with some of the characteristics associated with the most famous national parks around the world. When you think about your siblings and what experiences you had growing up, in a symbolic manner, which of the 12 National Parks (NP) listed here best describes your sibling relationship(s):

1. **Yosemite NP, California**—Best known for its waterfalls and towering granite monoliths – the most well-known being El Capitan. This national park gets symbolically aligned with the only child. (Because nothing stands out in this world like a 3,000-foot granite mountain that looks like it was cut in half.) As the only child, sometimes you feel like you might be out there all alone in the wilderness, but with your sturdy and strong constitution, many people are attracted to you and want to spend time with you.

2. **Serengeti NP, Tanzania Africa**—Although best known for its annual migration of zebras and wildebeests, the Serengeti hosts many families of animals presented here by their formal 'group' names: pride of lions, tower of giraffes, bloat of hippos, coalition of cheetahs, parade of elephants, and the aforementioned, dazzle of zebras and confusion of wildebeests. What do all of these groups of animals have in common? They are family oriented. They take care of one another because they know that outside forces are preying on them. It is a survival of the fittest world and to survive, they must stick together. Symbolically speaking, you and your siblings take care of one another and know how to survive together, often sticking together when facing the external world.

3. **Yellowstone NP, Wyoming**—Best known for its geothermal wonders including geysers, boiling mud volcanos, and hot springs amongst all of its historic wildlife. The only down side to Yellowstone is that these spectacular attractions are very spread out, often taking

two to four days to see all of them. Symbolically speaking, this means that your siblings (or family) are geographically dispersed, with a lot of physical distance between everyone; often months go by without being able to get together. However, every time you make the trek, it's worth the effort.

4. **Great Sand Dunes NP, Colorado**—Best known for being the largest sand box to play in, with the tallest dunes in North America, framed by a magnificent mountain range that rises from the high desert floor. This unique combination of elements creates extremely hot temperatures during the day and frigid cold temperatures by night and the fulgurites in the dunes creates extremely dangerous lightening scenarios as a lightning bolt can travel within the sand and then pop out unexpectedly miles away. Symbolically speaking, this means a family environment where your siblings are hot one minute, cold the next and sometimes dangerously charged. However, when the climate is just right, you play beautifully and have fantastic times together.

5. **Grand Canyon NP, Arizona**—Best known as a majestically deep and wide crevasse in the earth with amazing sunsets. Too distant and vast to hear from rim to rim; when someone speaks into the gorge, an echo is the only sound that returns. Symbolically speaking, this means that when you speak within your family, it seems like nobody hears you. The sound echoes back off the canyon walls but does not reach the other side. Furthermore, there is no bridge to close this gap, only a long arduous hike down and up the other side. If you're willing to make the trek, there may be a beautiful sunset or a mended relationship waiting for you.

6. **Everglades NP, Florida**—Best known for its ecological balance with many diverse species living together. It is the only place in the world where alligators and crocodiles exist side by side. It contains both temperate and tropical plant communities as well as marine and estuarine environments. Symbolically speaking, everyone in your family knows their place in balancing the system and can co-exist. But there is danger just under the surface of the water that could pop-up at any time.

7. **Denali NP, Alaska**—Best known for its vast wilderness, legendary wildlife, challenging conditions, and Mt. McKinley standing at 20,308 feet above sea level, rarely seen because of its relentless cloud cover. Symbolically speaking, although your family might be beautiful from a distance, it can be challenging and dangerous when you are together and you have been known to create harsh conditions for one another with a few sunny days sprinkled in.

8. **Galapagos Island NP**—Best known for its unique and rare aquatic species. Symbolically speaking, everyone in your family is a rare breed, special in your own ways, and each of you could be considered a different species. You may not be sure where you all came from but you swim together in the same currents.

9. **Arches NP, Moab, Utah**—Best known as a historical marvel with its delicate arches that were carved out over many centuries. Symbolizing the years of great history behind the making of your family but knowing that there is a delicateness that could crumble at any moment.

10. **Sequoia NP, California**—Best known for its Sequoias trees, which are some of the largest and oldest trees in the world. The largest being over 275 feet tall and 36 feet in diameter. As the second oldest national park, not much changes here. Symbolically speaking, same ole, same ole with your family. Like a grove of trees, you stand tall together and you are impressive as individuals, as well. As long as you keep the lumberjacks away!

11. **Bryce Canyon NP, Utah**—Best known for its bizarre shapes including slot canyons, windows, fins, and spires called "hoodoos." The most distinctive collection of rock spires (hoodoos) in the world. Symbolically speaking, are you still trying to figure out who is the favorite child in your family? One person thinks it's the other, while the other is thinking the same. In hoodoo world, everyone's the favorite child and all of the siblings believe that to be true of the other sibling(s).

12. **Manual Antonio NP, Costa Rica**—Best known for hosting one of the most beautiful beaches in the world and its numerous troops of monkeys that live simultaneously in the nearby jungle. Symbolically

speaking, a blended family where various troops have come together to live in what parents undoubtedly hope will be paradise. Have you ever held a juvenile howler monkey? Hair pulling and biting are the norm!

### Birth Order

Your Wildlife Viewing Scene also includes stores about your birth order. There are some exceptions worth mentioning before getting into typical birth order descriptions and how they affect money messages.

"Many things contribute to human behavior," says birth order expert Frank Sulloway, Ph.D. on Parents.com. "Birth order only explains a small chunk." Here are some other factors that alter traditional birth order roles.

**Gender.** Being born first doesn't necessarily guarantee firstborn status. In some cultures, a boy may be treated like a firstborn even when he has four older sisters, because he's the firstborn male.

**Special-needs sibling.** When a child is born with special needs, younger siblings may take on the firstborn role.

### Psychological Birth Order and Blended Families

Another resource states the difference between ordinal and psychological position in terms of birth order. According to a paper by Renee Devine of Adler Graduate School, "there is a difference between ordinal and psychological position within the family." Adler points out that "it is not the position to which the child is born into the family (the ordinal position) that has great significance on the personality; rather, it is the perception of the child as to their position in the family (psychological position). There are many factors, which could lead to an alternate position within the family than the one the individual is born into. One such factor is being a part of a blended family, which may have two separate groups of children." Another is large age gaps where younger siblings act more like only children or firstborns.

### Ordinal Birth Order

Typical birth order descriptions, referenced as the focused, striving firstborn, lost-in-thickets middleborn, and charismatic wild-child lastborn.

## Firstborns or the Oldest

The firstborn is the *only* child who has the full attention of the parent(s) and subsequently losing it to the second sibling. In this case, jealousy can become a guiding factor. Thus, a firstborn's aim is to please authority, to be seen as trustworthy. Firstborns are keen to achieve, they work hard, and they try to take up positions that will receive most praise, including taking up the mantle to shepherd and even bail younger siblings out of jams (regardless of the aforementioned jealousy). Thus, financial stability becomes paramount.

Statistically, more firstborns than you would imagine are company directors, presidents and prime ministers. According to a survey by CareerBuilder.com, firstborns are more likely to hold CEO, VP or senior management positions, and are most likely to earn $100,000 or more annually.

## Middleborns, or Middle

Middleborns often get along with everybody. They are usually born with similar age gaps on either side and their main aim is to make sure the waters run smooth. They are great in open-plan offices since they get along in groups, and it's a myth that they are the troubled dark characters (in fact, if anyone is going to go for psychological help it's typically the first or last born). That said, because their first concern is to make sure that everyone gets what *they* need, middleborns can lose their own sense of direction and lose themselves. Middleborns tend to pursue jobs that require excellent negotiating skills and are often in the helping or team-oriented professions such as nursing, law enforcement, teaching, firefighting or team athletes. Typically, they earn about $35,000 less than firstborns.

## Lastborn or Youngest

With a moniker like "the baby of the family" it's no wonder youngest children tend to be rebels, daredevils and clowns, in part because parents get more confident with every child and relax the rules. So, the lastborn are the most likely to make breakthroughs in creativity and science. They are the innovators and entrepreneurs. They end up either working to survive or as millionaires, and not much in between. They either hold more of the journalism and arts jobs or end up in sales, advertising, or entrepreneurs. Research has found that the youngest sibling in a family is more likely to take career risks... and thus, those who go this route, end up far more successful and more likely to be millionaires. This is because the youngest child has a natural tendency to test limits and rebel against norms.

## Only Child

The only child was once an anomaly because families were larger. Lots of people are now choosing to have just one child and pour all of their resources (hopes and dreams) into this person. Only children were often dubbed "lonely" and even "odd" in some cultures. Today more parents socialize the only child with other children and put them in activities like group sports so they get accustomed to teamwork and collaboration. Being an only child is often a great position to be in because confidence, independence, self-entertainment is part of the deal. They are generally very verbal and articulate as well. On the other hand, they may not adapt or cope as well as those from multi-sibling households in more chaotic situations, for instance, a loud and lively cubical environment or highly energetic work group. When it comes to career and compensation, only children are similar to firstborns, going for high-performing, high-paying, intellectual careers.

**Step 2. Story Sparks**

**Sibling Dynamics**

1. Which of the 12 National Park examples best describe your sibling dynamics and why?
2. If applicable, ask your sibling(s) which park(s) they would choose and why?
3. Up the ante (if possible). Ask your parents which park(s) they would choose to describe your family and why.
4. What strengths were present in your sibling relationships? If you had

no siblings, what were the advantages to that?

5.  What were the challenges you faced as a sibling or only child growing up in your household, and how did that directly affect your money messages?

6.  What money messages were present growing up with your family?

## Birth Order

1.  What is your birth order? How many siblings, stepsiblings, half-siblings were part of the household you grew up in?

2.  Do you relate best to your ordinal or a psychological birth order? (e.g., I was the youngest child until we became a blended family, then there were two rebels in the house because neither of us would give up the title of youngest, or I was the youngest, but there were many years between us so I behaved more like the oldest.)

3.  How does your birth order/only child impact your spending habits?

4.  How does your birth order/only child relate to your money messages?

## Step 3. Money Messages

Document and share your adventures, including the National Park that best represents your family. Summarize your money messages and key insights from your Wildlife Viewing Area (sibling dynamics) movie scene(s); remember to affirm, revise or eliminate these money messages accordingly.

### *Fellow Explorer: Mountaineer Matt at Wildlife Viewing Area* (Sibling Dynamics)

First of all, I relate most to the Galapagos National Park – each person in my family is unique.

My mom grew up in Rawlins, Wyoming, a dust bowl town, and my grandfather bought land that was then used to produce oil. After my grandparents died, my mom would receive an oil check of maybe $400 a month. That ran the budget for the house. With five kids, we didn't have a lot of money. You would go down for breakfast and all the good cereal was gone! Scarcity became a big theme.

## COURAGEOUS MONEY: YOUR ADVENTURE THROUGH MONEY NATIONAL PARK

We had to make certain choices and that is what framed our concept. We were given tools to go out and make money, like mowing lawns and washing dishes. Once I made my first paycheck, scarcity started to become abundance.

One of my first loves was music. If you listen to music, you hear the hook, feel the groove, drums speak to you, you always want to "hear the music." I would be over the moon buying records for $5 a piece. I mowed lawns and used the money to buy albums. When winter came, it would be shoveling snow. I built an album collection—My first investment! It had taken me a few years to get that collection to fifty albums. But then something happened, my brother, who was not a good brother, sold my albums for weed, so then I learned about loss.

*Money Message:* I would continue working hard and investing, but understand that it could be taken away. I would think about risk, reward and protection. I would think about who I could trust to be aware of the investment and fully recognize all the physical labor I went through to get to that point of investing. Asset allocation, diversity, making it a mathematical process instead of an emotional one, compounding and time in the market, are powerful tools to investments. You have to be willing to work hard, take risks, enjoy success and, at times, accept some loss.

# Adventure Scene #7: The Park Gift Shop

*Making and Spending Your Own Money*

*"Don't spend it all in one place." ~ Grandma*

## Step 1. Setting the Scene

The Park Gift Shop is all about what gifts you bought yourself because you finally had your own money to spend. It says a lot about how you first learned the value of a dollar and what money could do for you. Think about it. What do you recall about the first time you had your own money to spend on something important to you? How did it make you feel?

Outside of paying bills, chances are, somewhere along the way, you had the opportunity to earn and/or spend some money that you considered to be yours, "mad money" if you will, free of all expectations and especially those of family members. Having this luxury is both powerful and freeing. You may also discover that this power and freedom may have defined you in many ways. Before diving into your money stories about what you did with your allowance, earnings from your first job, and the first car that you purchased on your own, there is a concept that you should be aware of when it comes to shared money management: **Yours, Mine, Ours.** To understand this concept, take a look at the two overlapping circles.

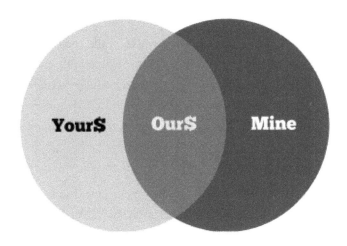

The tricky part is explaining these because 'Mine' is actually yours (the reader) and 'yours' means someone else other than you. Probably someone you live with or co-mingle funds with, such a family members or business partners. Ours is what is shared. Consider what "pools of funds" would be in each of the three areas (Yours, Ours, Mine) in your life: Think of any form of cash, investments, checking, savings, assets (e.g., a house), or additional resources such as a shared cellphone bill, vehicles, allowances, distributions, inheritance, trusts or a family business, you name it. If it has a monetary value, it fits somewhere on this diagram.

Let's say you are a teenager and you're making your own money. Is it truly in the "Mine" area? This means that you can do what you want with it, no strings attached, no expectations from your parents or anyone else, and no explanations needed. But if, for instance, you are on your parent's car insurance policy or phone bill and you share the payments, not all of your hard-earned money can go into 'Mine', some of it goes into 'Ours'. To elaborate, if any person with whom you co-mingle funds has a say in what is "yours," it's not yours, it's Ours!

Therefore, if neither party has free will to do what that they want with the pool of funds or portions of it, then it goes in the 'Ours' area. Ours means that before spending it, discussions and joint decisions are required and expectations must be clear from both parties regarding how these funds get used. Conversations typically do not happen around many monthly bills that get paid from the 'Ours' area; once the purchase is made, so are the assumptions about how it gets paid. Your Park Gift Shop stories will be focused exclusively on 'Mine'—Funds that are unequivocally yours with no strings attached. You can spend at will. The next adventure scene, Currency River, covers the 'Ours' bucket.

**Step 2. Story Sparks**

As with the other adventure scenes you have experienced so far, there are many story sparks here to choose from. Read through the various topics that apply to you and decide which ones you want to further develop as part of your movie. Topics at The Park Gift Shop include allowances, your first job, your financial IQ, your first car, home ownership, status symbols and your identity—all tied to money messages!

**Allowances**

1. What is your story regarding allowances growing up? Did you get one? How much? For what?
2. Did you consider your allowance to be a lot of money at the time?
3. What did you do with the money?
4. What were you allowed to do with "your" money? Any expectations?
5. Were there ways to make extra money around the house?
6. If you didn't get an allowance, how did you acquire things you wanted?
7. Who taught you/how did you learn basic money management skills?

# COURAGEOUS MONEY: YOUR ADVENTURE THROUGH MONEY NATIONAL PARK

## First job

1. Tell about your first job. How old were you? What was the job? What was your purpose for getting the job?
2. What were you allowed to or encouraged to do with the money you earned? What were you not allowed to do with "your" money?
3. What was your first major purchase? Did you save for it? What was the process of saving like and how long did it take? What did it mean to you when you purchased the thing you wanted?
4. How old were you when you got your first paycheck with taxes withheld? Do you recall your reaction when you saw how much went to taxes?
5. What is your money message around working?

## Financial IQ - Can you make money *and* manage it?

NBA legend, Shaquille O'Neal, spent over $1 million within sixty minutes of signing his first major contract. His financial advisor told him, "You were lucky enough to make it, but are you smart enough to keep it?"

He learned some lessons about money that day and immediately started making changes to his financial IQ. Today, he is Dr. Shaquille O'Neal and is a well-known franchise investor who is worth over $400 million, mostly due to his burger and pretzel franchises.

Warren Buffet, noted for his prudent investment strategy and frugal spending habits gives good advice, *"Don't save what is left after spending but spend what is left after saving."*

1. How do you balance making *and* managing money?
2. What is your financial strategy: balancing earning, spending, saving, giving and investing?
3. What is working for you or what do you want it to be?

## First car

A car says a lot about a person! For many, having their first car, especially one they paid for or contributed to, was a huge accomplishment and status symbol.

1. Share your story about your first car.
2. How did it come to be? Who paid for it?
3. Was it a status symbol? How did the car add to or take away from your social status?
4. Who paid for the insurance?
5. How were cars viewed in your house—Transportation, reward, earned, 16th birthday present, etc.?
6. What is your car philosophy: Buy new, lease, payments, buy used, paid in full, etc.?
7. If you were a teen without a car or without your own car, what was that like?
8. How does your car history (or lack of cars, maybe you grew up in a city and took public transit) fit into your money messages?

**Home ownership**

1. What is your home ownership story (your path to get there, homes owned over the years, etc.)?
2. What money messages and financial management lessons come from home ownership?
3. If you've chosen not to own a home, or otherwise cannot afford to buy a house, in what ways does that impact your life?
4. Any opinions that you want to share on owning vs. renting?
5. What is your view of mortgage loan terms and payments; do you prefer shorter-term loans with higher payments or lower payments with a longer term?
6. How is your home a part of your identity?

**Status symbols**

# COURAGEOUS MONEY: YOUR ADVENTURE THROUGH MONEY NATIONAL PARK

With money comes the perception/illusion of status. Most people have a status symbol, be it a car, job, income, house, clothes, jewelry, large family, certain friends, etc.

**My identity**

1. What is your personal status symbol of choice?
2. Who are you separate from your money?
3. How does money define you?
4. What other things in your life define you? What are you known for?
5. How do you deal with any inequities in what you make compared to others?

**Step 3. Money Messages**

Document and share your adventure. Summarize your money messages and key insights learned throughout these valuable times in your life and how they appeared as your Park Gift Shop movie scene(s); remember to affirm, revise or eliminate these money messages accordingly.

*Fellow Explorer: Venturous Vin at the Park Gift Shop*

We grew up in an affluent community, but it was supported by the big three automakers. Being the 1980s and a boy in Detroit, cars were a big deal. Believe it or not, you would be hard pressed to see Porsche, Ferrari, Lamborghini, or Maserati on any of those streets. The television shows and movies of the time were all about fast cars. *Miami Vice, Dukes of Hazard, Knight Rider, Magnum P.I.*, you name the show and chances are there was a great car featured in it. I was definitely affected by those programs.

Fashion was the same way as it played a unique character in the entertainment media. Films such as *Beverly Hills Cop* and *American Gigolo* made me long to live on Rodeo Drive cruising in a Mercedes 500SL convertible. If I named off many of my favorite films, they almost certainly have a sportscar in them, even if they are terrible movies. So, as a teenaged boy, I plotted that if I was able to put $1,000 in the bank each month in ten years, I would be able to buy a new Lamborghini Countach ($120,000). I constantly scoured used car lots for hidden gems and would take nightly cruises at 2:00 a.m. just to window shop at the only exotic dealerships, around forty-five minutes in one direction, or the Rolls Royce dealer thirty minutes the other way. Back then, Porsche was the only brand that had a presence in my hometown. One night, I found a 1988 Porsche 930 turbo slant nose worth $150,000 stashed in the backlot fenced off. I was in love. It would take more than a decade, but that would be my first exotic car, with the Ferrari Testarossa from *Miami Vice* next in line. Never got the Lambo though, and they cost almost one million today.

*Miami Vice's* Don Johnson wore Ray Ban sunglasses, Italian loafers with no socks and a gold Rolex President watch. He cruised the streets in a white Ferrari. This snapshot of Don Johnson was integral into the trajectory that my life took at a very early age and to this day. When I first started to make some real money, I wanted that Rolex President. So, my broker directed me to DuQuet Jewelers, a fifty-year-old fine jewelry retailer just a few miles away from my house. I walked in there with the Ray Bans and the loafers and an attitude, shooting off my mouth about how much money I had just made, and the reason for my call. Incidentally, I was driving the Mercedes 500SL from *American Gigolo*.

The owner escorted me back to the diamond room and regaled me with stories of the diamond and jewelry business. After several hours, I emerged from that room having made my first investment in the world of luxury; it took me several years to get my watch though. It occurred to me that there is far more prestige in owning the business that sells the Rolex than simply having the watch on your wrist. I realized then that I didn't want to just spend money on luxury goods I had coveted for so long. I wanted to own the businesses that sold them to everyone else.

*Money Message:* My key insight is linked to one of the three words that I used as my park entrance fee—Luxury. Money is what defines luxury for each and every person on earth. Most people believe that private jets, and sports cars, and mansions are a luxury and if you have the resources, they can become a reality. Some people on a different level think of a big screen tv and a new pickup truck or boat to take up to the lake as a luxury that many cannot afford. But there is also a segment of the population that find a warm dry blanket to sleep upon or a cold glass of clean water to drink a luxury. Money can be such a personal perspective for everyone.

That said, if I could be more courageous with one thing in my life when it comes to money, it would be around giving. Because I always feel like we are saving our pennies for the next deal, I am not as generous as I would like to be with others. While we do participate in a multitude of charity events around the world each year, I just wish I could do more personally. Throughout the last decade, my responsibility to the business and its supporters has grown. I no longer feel like it is appropriate to live in such a lavish and loud manner, especially while others are having such a hard time.

# Adventure Scene #8: Currency River

**Currency River**

*"Money may not buy love, but fighting about it will bankrupt your relationship."*
*~Michelle Singletary*

Have you ever thought about the word, currency? Depending on the source, the word currency is derived from a variety of Latin, middle English and Anglo-French words all spelled similarly, and which mean "running, flowing, moving along." The terminology and references between money (currency) and water are limitless. Consider the following: stream of income, cash flow, liquidity event, dot-com bubble, down the drain, and pool of money. At Currency River, we are going to explore how money flows like a river to and through your households and influences your relationships.

While Currency River was designed with couples in mind, there are plenty of elements that apply to those without a partner. The idea of a widow comes to mind, where her children (heirs) step in to serve as her financial advisors.

Another example might be family members who have shared assets (business, vacation home, timeshare, etc.). Those who need to come together on a regular basis to make money-related decisions. Even besties and singles with roommates can explore this stop in the park!

Regardless of your relationship status, don't let the design of this scene keep you from exploring the parts that apply to your life.

## Step 1. Setting the Scene

Recalling the Yours, Mine, and Ours diagram described in *The Park Gift Shop*, Currency River focuses exclusively on the 'Ours' section. This is where joint discussions are required, and there are expectations from both parties regarding how co-mingled funds/assets get used. Regardless of who does or doesn't work or who brings in the most money, successful couples plan together, budget together, give together, spend together and save together.

### Family relations and money messages

Why do couples argue? Top three reasons: children, sex and MONEY! During a money argument, how often do you think about or explore key money messages associated with your everyday behaviors that are being attacked, triggered or discussed in your arguments? Think about it; if you argue about money, do you ever stop to explore key fundamental differences in each of your money messages—the very beliefs that are driving many of your adult behaviors and quite possibly these arguments? Have you ever worked with a therapist? Did your therapist ever explore with you the relationship you have with money, or how it ties to your values and beliefs, then connect the dots to how your money message are impacting your relationship? If money is the "root of all evil," then what role does money play in a challenging relationship?

Consider this scenario: Couples bring rarely explored or discussed deeply rooted money messages into a relationship with one another. Keeping in mind, at one time each partner was likely an independent, financially self-sufficient person or capable of being one. Yet, by virtue of being in the relationship with each other, each person takes on stereotypical roles or adapt to one or the other's style. In this example, let's say one person ends up more the financial subordinate. This can lead to conflict because again, the subordinate person was once confident and self-sufficient. Such subordination erodes confidence and trust and creates dependency, which can lead to arguments. Yet, creating a partnership, where financial roles are interchangeable and knowledge, skills, and abilities are equalized between parties is often too ideal of a goal to achieve for many. So, where do you start?

## Money Roles

Money Roles are all about power and control over money within relationships (family/spousal/partnerships) and between households. Power and control can mean one's access to money, use of money, control of money, and money management. Seeking a balance of power was discussed back at Gender Mountain, where you learned that over time, each person will 'seek to own or control something' to find balance within themselves and within a relationship.

Relating specifically to money and relationships, a money bridge may help to identify the various roles that people adopt.

## The Money Bridge

# COURAGEOUS MONEY: YOUR ADVENTURE THROUGH MONEY NATIONAL PARK

The words used at both ends of the bridge are harsh on purpose because we want people to move toward the middle, away from these roles. To the extreme: The Controller is the one in the house wanting to manage all of the financial matters, to be the breadwinner or the only source of income and the one who directs *all* of the money-related activities (knowing who to contact, what accounts exist, when things are due, where to find everything, why things are set up the way they are, budget management, overall purchasing approval, and how to access accounts). The Victim, by choice or by circumstance, is then left standing alone on the other end of the bridge, often in the dark; not having any knowledge about the who, what, when, where, why or how. The Victim is clueless about their financial picture. All too often, when a family member assumes the Controller role, another family member is forced to balance the scale by taking the Victim role. Being the Victim creates total dependency by fostering a feeling of helplessness and fearfulness around financial matters (and probably other things). This can leave the Victim paralyzed, mentally wounded and easy prey when/if the Controller is no longer in the picture. If the Controller dies suddenly, the Victim may be helpless to understand how to manage their finances going forward. Sometimes the pendulum swings and overspending may become the norm instead. To step out of the Victim and Controller roles requires a *willingness to be vulnerable*. The Victim needs to find the courage to start asking and/or seeking more information while the Controller needs to see that there is power in teaching others, and that it's okay to let go of some of the control. If the Victim is hesitant to learn; Controllers can choose to help reduce some dependency by acknowledging the Victim's fears, seeking to understanding their hesitation, recognizing some of the self-limiting money message beliefs that are in-play and acknowledging that both people play a role in changing this scenario for the better. Easier said than done, yes. But anything worth something takes awareness and effort.

As we move away from the extremes of Controller and Victim, we slide into those in the Provider and Follower roles. The Provider is typically the one to make many of the financial decisions, but this person knows the value and necessity of making sure the Follower is in the know, informed and involved in some capacity. This is often a mutually beneficial agreement whether by design or by accident. At a minimum, people in the Follower role should know how to access joint accounts and have some basic working financial knowledge. Followers should seek to become more competent in their basic money management skills and financial IQ. The goal here is to achieve a sense of self-confidence to the degree that they could step in when and where needed, especially in the case of an emergency or life-altering event, and with some level of comfort. *It's okay to be a Follower*; just be an informed Follower. That way, if life takes an unexpected turn, you are prepared and can save yourself a great deal of heartache and protect yourself from fraud (criminals prey on the uninformed)! The Provider has a responsibility too, in helping the Follower become more confident! The Provider's role should be that of a teacher; a financial leader who shares relevant information and knowledge with those impacted by the financial relationship. More about how to develop one's financial IQ and financial self-confidence were provided in Part I.

While some relationships remain balanced at Provider and Follower 'until death do us part', we believe the *ideal role* for relationships is the center of the bridge, the Partnership. We do not assume that you have to join all of your accounts or have access to all of each other's financial endeavors and balance sheets to be successful, but you do need to be able to communicate openly and both parties need to be confident in their abilities to handle and manage money! From basic cash-flow management (budgeting) to understanding retirement accounts. This does not mean that both people need to pay the bills or manage the family's cash flow simultaneously; it simply means that both people know *how* to do these things, and understand what is required to keep things moving seamlessly if and when needed.

Regardless of whether or not you pool your funds, in a Partnership, both parties feel comfortable talking about money and having money conversations (known as psychological safety-the ability to say or ask anything without fear of judgment or repercussions). They have peace of mind around their money competencies and are knowledgeable of their financial and estate plans. One client once used the term, "croak book" to describes the document that was prepared for the family in case of an emergency—A book that informed the family of advisors, where to find essential documents and/or accounts, passwords, will, stock certificates, etc. In other words, the playbook for survivors. As you evaluate your relationships with others, tied together with the flow of money, having a Partnership requires trust and ultimately creates self-confidence, self-worth and self-esteem; a healthy ebb and flow for both parties.

## Step 2. Story Sparks

1. How do you think your place on the bridge relates to your earliest memories of money, money messages or your money mindset?
2. If you share assets or finances with anyone (spouse, partner, family members or friends), which role (from the money bridge) do you play in each of these relationships?
3. Is there a role imbalance? What is your part in perpetuating a problem of imbalance?
4. How might you be contributing to keeping someone in the Victim role—Even if you think you're doing it to be helpful or rescue them from discomfort?
5. How do you control money (or not) in your relationships?
6. What excuses are at each end of the bridge (Victim/Controller)?
7. What excuses do you make?
8. What courage is needed to do what's right?
9. What do you see as your roles and responsibilities regarding money?
10. How can you educate yourself and be more confident with or without the support of your partner/spouse/family?
11. What does the ultimate money-partnership relationship look like for you?
12. In what ways do you encourage/support other people in your life (partner, spouse, children, employees) to excel when it comes to money and finances?
13. What things do you need to share (knowledge, information, etc.) with others in your life to ensure that they are financially capable and confident if something happens to you?

## Emotional Impact

1. What emotions might be associated with where you are on the bridge?
2. What concerns or fears do you have around money and money management?
3. Guilt and shame are often associated with money and the various roles, most notably with the Victim role. Do you feel guilt or shame with regard to money?
4. How often do you talk about money or share aspects of your financial life with your partner? What about family, children, close friends, etc.?
5. How do you react/feel/respond if your shared financial arrangements are controlled by others?

## Step 3. Money Messages

Document and share your adventure. Summarize your money messages and key insights from your Currency River movie scene(s); remember to affirm, revise or eliminate these money messages accordingly.

### Fellow Explorer: Power-of-the-Purse Gina and Daring Denise at Currency River

**Power-of-the-Purse Gina:** I was voluntarily in the Victim role until my husband's dad died tragically. At that sudden turn of events my husband had to take over the family business. Now, I'm happy to be in the Follower role, much more informed and in the know about the household finances. My husband is now less in the Controller role—A role he assumed based on a lifetime of adopted money messages and assumed gender roles of needing to be the breadwinner—He has consciously moved into the provider role and has been my teacher.

*Money Message:* I would have set out to have a Partnership at the beginning of my marriage if I had been more aware. I got into credit problems early as the ultimate shopper, but I feel so empowered now. I do not want my kids to assume the role of Victim. They are learning from us now and see us operating as partners in our financial matters.

# COURAGEOUS MONEY: YOUR ADVENTURE THROUGH MONEY NATIONAL PARK

**Daring Denise:** Finance and money dictate a lot of things that you don't know have a correlation. My husband and I operated as partners from the beginning, we both went to college, he graduated with two degrees, and we both worked really hard.

I realized that I had literally lived to work my whole life. I've never not had a job. Working saved my life and I thrived at it. I operated on a fear that I wouldn't have enough money to pay the bills. And, although I was successful as a bank employee, I had an awakening along the way; my husband was managing all of our personal finances. I trust my husband, so that was not the issue. The awakening came from the fact that I was financially savvy, worked for a bank, a really smart person and yet I knew nothing about my personal finances! I guess it was just easier for him to take the lead in managing our money and I never thought to get involved. He works for the government, so I realized that if something happened to him, I would be clueless where to find everything and how to access it. That quickly changed and my husband was happy to share everything I needed to know. Now we share this role together.

*Money Message:* Even if you are financially savvy, it is easy to let someone else take the lead in managing your finances. Don't be caught off guard, both people in a relationship should be involved and in the know.

# Adventure Scene #9: Life Falls

*"We are all broken. That's how the light gets in." ~Ernest Hemingway*

**Step 1. Setting the Scene**

Simply stated, LIFE HAPPENS! And when it does, it affects our relationship with money. Think about what money messages you have learned by watching life happen to others or by what you experienced personally. Really stop and consider this one.

Life Falls refers to when any of the following life-changing events occur and more specifically, what happens to the survivors and/or the person(s) directly impacted by the event. In general, Life Falls are those things that can throw you off balance and make you feel like you are tumbling down Niagara Falls in a rickety old barrel! In some cases, they include unexpected changes, new beginnings or simply a change in your life's status quo going forward. Life falls includes:

- Death of a loved one
- Divorce or permanent break-ups (including friendships)
- Closing a business
- Job loss or working in an industry that is becoming obsolete
- Retirement
- Job relocation, out of preference or necessity
- Job change
- Cognitive changes that can affect lifestyle: Dementia, Alzheimer's
- Life changing or long-term recovery from an illness or accident
- Impacts to one's cash flow, budget, cost of living, or lifestyle
- Economic fears, downturns, recessions, depressions, inflation, or any threat to ones' ability to cover their basic needs: food, clothing, shelter.
- In 2020-2021, there were some additional major Life Falls events:
- The COVID-19 pandemic (illness, death, anti-mask and anti-vax protests, long-haulers, overworked healthcare workers and essential workers, and the economic roller coaster)
- The most controversial U.S. Presidential election in our time in which, the highest number ever of people voted
- Protests for racial justice and equality
- American citizens stormed the U.S. Capitol building as a result of rioting and claims of election fraud
- Mass shootings in Atlanta and Boulder
- Major weather disasters such as the greatest number of hurricanes ever in the Atlantic to come on-shore in the U.S.; Texas and other states literally frozen over in winter storms that caused mass destruction, long-term power-outages, and significant financial distress.
- Election of the first female, Black and Asian American Vice President of the United States.
- Record time high unemployment rate, record stock market highs and lows, crude oil bottomed out, trillions in pandemic relief dollars being spent, and some of the lowest interest rates available in years resulting in one of the biggest housing booms in U.S. (We are still waiting for the aliens.)

The only constant is change.... In the harshest of these scenarios, when it comes to telling your money message story, it might be easy to get caught up in the details of the situation, the gut-wrenching emotion and the devastation caused. While these all make for good movies and are all critical pieces to your story, we want to encourage you *focus on the impact* that these events had on you (and others around you). How did the event(s) impact your money messages, for instance, and were there financial lessons learned?

You may recall reading about how values and emotions are directly tied to money fears and uncertainty in *Part I: When Money Talks.* The connections are deep. And you may also want to consider revisiting your Money Mindset: Saver, Spender, Investor and Giver and connect the dots between the values associated with each of the mindsets and what impact a Life Falls event has them. It's easy to see how some Life Falls events can shake people all the way to their core values!

Most of us would rather stand atop or below the falls enjoying the scenery and the rainbows in the mist. We rarely expect to go over the falls in a major way, life spiraling out of control! Who could blame us for wanting to live in denial because we could not control the situation or because we didn't know it was coming? There is no way we could adequately prepare for that kind of fall. As a result, we become afraid, scared, fearful and anxious—Paralyzed. We do everything in our power to try to prevent bad things from happening and yet, they do. It is ok to grieve what we can't control, but then, we must find ways to cope and hopefully thrive again. This exercise can help.

As an example, consider for a moment how you felt during the pandemic: It may have been more like a series of waterfalls or rapids, and they came with relatively little warning. Once it hit in earnest, we were stunned into submission, at first, then the civil disobedience began and the numbers climbed. After a few months, everyone thought it was safe to find some sense of new normalcy; but protests, hurricanes, the election and winter holidays brought it to a raging tumultuous boil again. This time, worse. Then the vaccine, and hope! More and more vaccines were given and at the same time the mask mandates were dropped, businesses were re-opened and then spring break was upon us again. Kids went crazy partying like it's 1999 in Miami, ignoring curfews. Add to that the stress between friends and family. Some separated for over a year and for others, "What pandemic?" It was a year of judgement and coping. A time like this can set you off balance, not knowing where to turn from one moment to the next. Nor knowing who to trust and where to find solace or validation. Not having the comfort of your family nearby perhaps, or the realization that life may not be "normal" again for a very long time: *This* is Life Falls!

This is also why we get so emotional about money. When we go over Life Falls, we are rarely prepared for the financial impact that it has on us, any more than we are prepared for the event itself. Such uncertainties elicit fear.

## Step 2. Story Sparks

To tell your story here, the questions are designed to focus on how Life Falls events have impacted you directly. At one point we would have said that if you haven't experienced a Life Falls event consider yourself lucky, and to draw from those you have observed. But given the pandemic, we have all now experienced at least one Life Falls event.

1. What Life Falls event(s) have you faced or witnessed?
2. What challenges did you face as a result of these events?
3. What values were messed with when things got out of control?
4. What money messages were tweaked?
5. What fears or anxieties do you have about your future financial security since the event(s)?
6. How have you managed a financial crisis in the past?
7. How can you apply what you learned then, to now?
8. How does job insecurity or market volatility cause challenges or anxiety for you or your household?
9. What Life Falls events have moved you to action in terms of better money management? What lessons did you learn from this?
10. Were there any tragedies that led to money challenges?
11. What were the hidden blessings in your Life Falls event(s)?

## Step 3. Money Messages

Document and share your adventure. Summarize your money messages and key insights from your Life Falls movie scene(s); remember to affirm, revise or eliminate these money messages accordingly.

### *Fellow Explorer: Mountaineer Matt at Life Falls*

As a financial planner, what I try to get people to think about with their finances is abundance rather than scarcity. My call to clients at the start of the pandemic was, don't jump off the ledge because markets come back. In one day, I talked ten people off the ledge, but I had three clients who sold everything in March 2020 when the market hit a historic low. I was devastated. I tried every angle of advice. I asked for one more week, but people in that fear-driven spot get blinders on and can't think of anything on the peripheral or outside. Then I'm charged with picking up the pieces.

*Money Message:* One of my 3 words was tragedy. I see tragedy with people who panic when the market crashes; I see it when people don't save enough; and when people are not prepared when something impacts their world. My goal as a financial planner is to help people make good investment decisions so they are safe in areas such as health and the care of their health as well as being knowledgeable about their finances. If I could rewrite my movie scene here, I would be seen instructing all of my clients to do nothing at the onset of a pandemic, and they would all listen!

There will always be tragedy, or Life Falls. Being emotionally stable and not worrying about money all the time is critical for health and wellbeing. And having the ability to create abundance. To achieve a goal, it may mean spending more time in the office for one person. For someone else, it may mean taking on a side gig. How can you afford the experiences you want? Be creative and put effort into it. This is freedom, one of my 3 words, and money provides the independence so you can do what you want; in my case, create experiences. Seek freedom.

# Adventure Scene #10: Tall Tales Campground

**Tall Tales Campground**

*"The most courageous act is still to think for yourself. Aloud." ~Coco Chanel*

**Step 1: Setting the Scene**

These are the stories that can't be fabricated! They are your money secrets; your action-adventure movie bloopers and outtakes. The ones that you don't readily share with everybody and may not be brave enough to put in your movie. Money stories are *deep* and some of them are so deep that they have never been shared with anyone...ever. Until now.

The scene at Tall Tales Campground is where you tell your most outrageous money stories—think ghost stories from around the campfire as a kid—except these will be true. Embarrassing, heart-breaking, morally wrong, unethical, shameful or hilarious as they might be. Like how you used money to survive crazy things that you did when you were young or stunts that you may not be so proud of today. To lighten the load, we know that many people have crazy stories to share, so you are not the first young person to shoplift ten tubes of Bonny Bell lip balm because you couldn't decide which one to buy. Please tell your stories with humor and lighten your load. You, and only you get to decide whether you share them with anyone else. Don't worry. Your secrets are safe with us!

## Step 2. Story Sparks

Let's have some fun and put these stories out there. You may already know the story you want to share. If not, read through the following to see if any apply to you. Have you ever...

1. Left the store and realized that you didn't pay for an item, like that hat on your head or the ten pounds of potatoes hidden on the bottom of your shopping cart? What did you do?
2. Used your school lunch money for something other than lunch?
3. How about used any money for something other than what was intended (e.g., buying an ATV with scholarship money)?
4. When someone else provided the money to buy something, did you pocket the change?
5. Have you ever shoplifted?
6. "Borrowing" a little money from around the house: Dad's wallet, Mom's purse, the coin jar, the family safe, or a hidden cash stash?
7. Sold something that wasn't yours to sell, or maybe something behind your parent's or sibling's back?
8. Regifted a gift that someone else gave to you, pretending it was new?
9. Using company resources or corporate discounts for personal gain?
10. What is your Tall Tale story?

## Step 3. Money Messages

Document and share your adventure; this is optional for Tall Tales Campground (your secrets can remain buried if you'd like), but you should at least capture your key money messages learned and insights. Include any residual emotions or resolutions as a result of these actions and remember to affirm, revise or eliminate these money messages accordingly.

# COURAGEOUS MONEY: YOUR ADVENTURE THROUGH MONEY NATIONAL PARK

## *Fellow Explorer: Carefree Candi at Tall Tales Campground*

My mother's first husband was a bank robber and set an example for his two sons, my two half-brothers, who became chronic shoplifters, stealing everything from collectible comic books and antiques, to lawn mowers from home and garden stores. They always got away with it! Growing up watching their example, I never wanted to spend my money on (or steal!) objects, but I became an instant sucker for lavish experiences and the memories with others that would ensue. One time, I spent my rent money that I had earned serving at a restaurant over the holidays (busiest time in fine dining...cha-ching!), on a surprise birthday party for my girlfriend at The Cincinnatian Hotel and invited ten of her friends. I got sick that night on the lobster and champagne. That's what I get for being irresponsible with my hard-earned money, but it was so fun!

*Money Message:* I could have paid my rent on time and worked extra hours to have the same experience—with proper planning and not acting on impulse. My key insights; enjoy experiences, live for them! But plan ahead of time and have a separate account or rewards card dedicated to these special events.

# Adventure Scene #11: Shooting Stars

*"To be a star, you must shine your own light, follow your path, and don't worry about the darkness, for that is when the stars shine brightest."* ~Ralph Waldo Emerson

### Step 1. Setting the Scene

The camera zooms out to you, gazing up into the clear night sky in Money National Park, searching for your favorite constellations, discovering new ones and hoping to see a shooting star or better, a meteor shower or the northern lights!

Contemplate your adventure through Money National Park and think about your *Courageous Money* movie; your favorite scenes, new discoveries, and if you saw a shooting star—New insights that allowed you to see how your behaviors are related to your money messages or even a new perspective on a shared scene.

# COURAGEOUS MONEY: YOUR ADVENTURE THROUGH MONEY NATIONAL PARK

## ...Fast Forward!

Congratulations! Now that your movie premier is over, you have been invited to join the Today Show to share your experience. On the show, the host ask you a few questions. You respond to the following:

1. Your Courageous Money movie is a masterpiece. Where did you get such great stories for each of the scenes?
2. What was your favorite or most memorable scene?
3. If you openly shared different perspectives of the same scene with someone, do you have new insights?
4. What was your favorite twist or turn in the movie?
5. What was your favorite triumph or overcoming a challenge scene?
6. What do you think of your ending? Could it have ended differently? How/Why?
7. Just curious, did you notice a theme of food, the relationship with food, or did the consumption of food surface in your movie scenes? What connections between food and money are true for you?

As they soak in your answers, they ask you one, final, surprise question: "Would you be willing to create one more scene in your movie just for us?" You say, "Of course!" and they ask the key questions for this scene:

*"If money were a person sitting next to you at the dinner table, what conversation would you have with money? What would you say to money and what would money say back to you?" You reply...*

# Conclusion: Changing the way we talk about money, one story at a time.

Money is still the #1 taboo topic within households. The purpose of this action-adventure movie through Money National Park was to get you to 1) Discover where your relationship with money came from, 2) Understand how your money messages drive the majority of your behaviors and choices as an adult, and 3) Let go of money messages that are no longer serving you in favor of the ones that are, and find the courage to start talking about money.

It is a choice to be informed and in the know about financial matters. Even if someone controls the finances in your world, now is the time to edit that scene. Start today! All scenes are imaginable in Money National Park. A scene change is not about forcing your truth on someone else regarding different perspectives of the same movie scene. You both get to own your truths. Similarly, it is not about taking over control and displacing someone's money management role, it is the beauty of the *and*, where both people in the partnership can be involved and in the know at the same time. There is room for everyone to be financially savvy.

A special note to women: Do not let the norms of the past (or the present) dictate your relationship with money! Be courageous in your pursuit of financial security and be curious in learning how to make it happen. Let *nothing* stop you. *You are worth it!*

This adventure was designed as a fun and innovative way to provide you with a language that you can use in having more comfortable money conversations. Start by telling stories! By creating your own *Courageous Money* movie, with each adventure scene specifically designed by you to elicit more insight into your money-related behaviors and discover where your deeply engrained money messages came from, you now have plenty of stories to share! By using this book, as well as additional resources found at MoneyNationalPark.com, you now have the tools to mutually share stories with others. Money stories don't have to be about amounts and bank accounts and budgets. They are memories. In the end, the goal of this personal adventure through Money National Park was to change the way we talk about money...one story at a time.

Come visit anytime! Happy Trails!

# PART III. THE AUTHORS' COURAGEOUS MONEY MOVIES

# Amy's Adventure Movie Through Money National Park

*"Some people are so poor, all they have is money." ~Bob Marley*

As I sit here in the theatre with my name on the marquis, watching scenes that taught me the value of money, I know that my family members will be sitting in their own theatres, watching the exact same scenes; and we may not recognize it as one in the same.

As you read my story, you will see the value in having money conversations and sharing your money-movie with others. I was brave enough, because of this book, to share parts of my movie with my parents. While listening to their perspectives; I now have more accurate information to go on that has altered my perceptions, however, these clips still represent my unfiltered view:

### Park Entrance Fee

The three words that I think of when I hear the word money are: Freedom, Adventure and Hard-work. Or Use. Your. Wings.

### Money Mindset Mine

My money mindsets are Spender and Investor thus, I have an aggressive investment portfolio. My movie scene would be of Cindy and me investing $50,000 in a friend's business (a year's salary) and then seeing him drive up in a Jaguar a few months later, while we stand gob-slapped in disbelief, knowing it was our hard-earned money that bought it! Shiver me timbers!

*Money Message:* I have to spend money to make money! What I need to learn is that what seems too good to be true, often is! Deep down, I knew better than to invest with a friend, but I didn't have the courage to say no. If I could, I would rewrite my movie scene with me saying, "No thanks," to that opportunity of a lifetime with a flash-forward scene showing us driving that jag instead!

## Fountain of Youth

As youngsters, my sisters and I worked all summer helping Dad with his on-the-side landscaping business. Jokingly, I now call it child labor! We often worked 12-hour days in the Minnesota sweltering heat, all for $1 an hour—It was brilliant because by putting us to work he knew where we were all day while he was at work. At the end of each summer, I recall giving dad a tally of 180-200 hours, depending on the year. We kids really looked forward to getting paid for our long summer's work. Then one year, we didn't get paid. We were hurt and angry. I recall being very disappointed that someone that I trusted would do this to us. We asked multiple times to get paid before we stopped asking. I remember how hard it was for us young girls to ask a parent for money that we had already earned. I truly don't recall if we ever got paid for that summer. But I recently worked up the courage to discuss this movie scene with my dad and step-mom. I was surprised and relieved to hear clips of the same scenes from their perspective. Apparently, there was a thing called billing or invoicing (as kids we weren't a part of this process). So, before we could get paid, Dad had to get paid. One year there was a delay in payment from the client and he did not have enough in reserves to cover us. As a child, I never knew this was happening behind the scenes. I was initially concerned about sharing this story, but my parents encouraged me to tell if from my perspective. It was very validating.

As an adult, my dad has taught me many lessons in being financially smart and I still love our regular financial strategy conversations.

This one early memory from my childhood helped lay the foundation for who I am today; a wealth creator, not dependent upon anyone for my livelihood.

*Money Message:* (1) Taking a quote from Cindy's grandmother, "I can do it myself!" and; (2) There are three sides to every money story: yours (in this case my dad's), mine, and my sister's.

## Gender Mountain

When I was finishing up graduate school the professor had each student sit in a chair in front of the rest of the class to learn to receive feedback. Our classmates were instructed to share with us anything they saw that could interfere with us being a successful consultant. Our response to each comment was limited to two words, "Thank You!" For my first two pieces of feedback I received, "You're young!" (I was 26) and then, "You're female!" (Yes, that was true, too). I replied, "Thank you" to both and thought to myself, "I'll work on that!" My takeaway? I couldn't wait until I turned 40, but I'm still female. Did these two factors affect my career? I would bet they did. But more importantly, I didn't focus on the glass ceiling or the brick wall right in front of me. I persevered by climbing new ladders or searching until I found the end of that brick wall and then simply walked around it. I may have missed a promotion, salary increase or opportunity along the way because I was "young and female," but what I learned that day sitting in front of my classmates was priceless, "Feedback is the gift of fruitcake! Sometimes life gives you dried-up tasteless commentary, take what you want and discard the rest."

*Money Message:* Just because someone tells you something, doesn't mean they are right or that you have to embody it. One of my clients recently said, "What other people think of me is no business of mine." I love that saying. If I listened to every piece of criticism everyone in the last 55 years has doled out to me, I'd curl up in a ball. Instead, I take what I want and leave the rest. I find a way to make things happen despite the obstacles in front of me because I believe I *can*. Same when it comes to money. I can make it, spend it and make more.

### Generation Trail

I'm a Gen Xer. I'm self-reliant, an entrepreneur, and very independent. With a wandering soul and a creative mind, I would shrivel and die without a flexible work environment! With divorced parents, I was raised by Gilligan's Island; coming home every day and watching those stranded castaways try to get off the island. I never could figure out why they tried so hard to leave that beautiful place or why Mrs. Howell packed so much for a three-hour tour!

Day after day, I was on my own or getting into trouble with my sisters. As a rebel child, I know that I was a challenge to raise. If you hang out in my movie theatre long enough, you would see a lot of crazy, adventurous, outrageous and ingenious things happening and often wonder, "How on earth did she survive that one?" While in my parent's theatres you might first notice their gray hair followed by many lessons on how to raise mischievous, risk-taking children. Sorry Mom for messing up your cast-iron skillet in the sand dunes with Heidi, and Dad, sorry for dismantling the lawnmower carburetor to use the parts in my go-cart—but at least putting it back together got me out of a day of landscaping.

As for fitting in, it never happened; I wasn't sure where I belonged throughout my life – another Gen Xer trait. I live with an eternal "This isn't it" perspective. So, I guess it shouldn't be a surprise that in the two decades that Cindy and I have been together, we have owned 8 properties, all in different locations, including an oceanfront condo on Isla Mujeres, Mexico that at one time we thought would be our forever home. But in our lives, "forever" is relative... And you thought only Ellen DeGeneres bought a new house every year! The only thing that doesn't change regularly are our cars and our love for each other.

*Money Messages:* As a Gen Xer, I have a few: (1) There's a fine line between risk-taking and reckless –I like to take risks. And while that is true, in adulthood they are often more calculated than they were in my youth, which looked more like sledding off the roof our garage; (2) My money motto: Work hard and play harder! Enjoy life, you only live once; (3) Use your wings—to soar or to get out there and make some money!

## Culture Crater

I officially came out as being gay to my family around 2002. I was climbing the corporate ladder and becoming a successful professional. During this time, I divorced my husband and wanted to let my dad know that my next relationship would be of the alternative lifestyle (words used around that time to describe being gay or lesbian). His reply was quick, "Well, there goes your career!" For a moment I was shocked, but then it opened my eyes to what I might be up against working in a "man's world," the predominantly older white male banking environment. Fortunately, it didn't affect my career and today my dad is one of our biggest fans. Cindy and I are blessed in that all of our family members embrace and love us.

# COURAGEOUS MONEY: YOUR ADVENTURE THROUGH MONEY NATIONAL PARK

Although being a lesbian may not have impacted my career, I fear my fashion choices could have done some damage. Thankfully, Cindy has been my stylist for the last many years and often said that we should invent "Garanimals" for adults; she means for the fashion challenged, like me. I might be slim but I'm not the best model—not being the stereotypical female high-heeled, skirt-wearing type, I'm proud to call my comfortable pair of black, thick-soled, patent leather, Paul Green $300 designer shoes—that I got on-sale, my "lesbian stilettos."

*Money Message:* Be authentic to yourself. I'm Amy the professional leader who happens to be gay, not Amy the lesbian. People can't help but put labels on you, but you can help reshape them into something you are proud of, because the L-word isn't a bad word! And yes, there are still many inequities for the LGBTQ+ community when it comes to professional careers. We have come a long way, but we still have a long way to go. Good news, the internet doesn't discriminate against anyone wanting to learn better financial management skills.

My second movie clip at Culture Crater occurs during my childhood. I watched my parents go through a Kramer vs Kramer divorce. My mom, who struggled financially afterward, lived in an apartment and could barely pay the rent. For Christmas, she could only afford to give us each a package of three colored underwear and three T-shirts. Both practical gifts; the T-shirts were to keep us warm and the underwear to prevent us from wearing holey underwear in the case of an emergency. Nonetheless, I recall watching my mom cry, knowing that she wanted to give us more each Christmas. To complicate matters, we had the comparison of my dad and step-mom's version of Christmas. You see, my step-mom's love language is gifts, and to this day, she loves to give thoughtful gifts to everyone she knows and loves. It's in her DNA. As kids, we benefited from this passion. At Christmas the expansive farm house living room floor would be filled with beautifully wrapped packages that would take hours to devour. Incredible gifts like an air hockey table, great games, toys, outdoor gear, sporting goods, clothes, shoes and boots. My all-time favorite was a pair of Rossignol skis that I was tricked into finding by going on a scavenger hunt into the creepy, spider-filled basement to retrieve. Of course, as a child, I loved all of the presents! But I remember my mom's pain just the same. I recall the inequity between the two households like it was yesterday. It also highlighted for me the difference between a single vs double income home.

As part of the courageous conversation that I recently had with my dad and step-mom (as a result of writing this book), I learned that the infamous gift shopper (my step-mom) had a Christmas savings account that she funded with a small amount being taken out of each of her paychecks (only *after* she funded her 401K, she was sure to tell me), and her shopping starting in July! She would use her lunch hours to start bargain hunting for Christmas presents. My skis were purchased from a friend's outdoor gear shop for $80 and a snowsuit could be purchased on the clearance sale rack in July for $8.00!

*Money Message:* To this day gift giving is not my love language, maybe for obvious reasons, or maybe it never was. I learned as a child and especially as a college student, the difference between needs and wants; to only buy what I needed and if I wanted something more, I needed to work more. Work equals money! I recently saw a small sign on someone's kitchen counter, "Dreams work when you do." It spoke to me!

### Wildlife Viewing Area (Sibling Dynamics)

What national park best represents my family? Manual Antonio NP, Costa Rica! Various troops of monkeys living together in one large jungle. My birth order: youngest child, or so I thought. At about age 10 we became a blended family with the addition of a step-mom and two step-sisters; one older, one younger. The troop got bigger and I had competition on my hands over being the youngest! My step-sister won the official role, but I did retain many of the youngest child traits: rebel, daredevil, confident, creative, innovator and entrepreneur.

But my movie scene is not about being the rebel child, rather it's about college planning. College was not assumed or discussed in our family. In fact, no family member from my parent's generation or before, or my expansive family of cousins, had graduated from college. I was born into the working class, my grandfather made it to 5th grade before becoming an ironworker for life and my other grandfather was an HVAC specialist.

My movie scene is a clip of me watching my dad and step-mother pay for my step-sister's college, while I worked full-time and went to school full-time for 9 years, paying for my own college education... Again, everyone's movie is different. I was in for another eye-opener when I talked with my step-mom about this recently. I found out that the money given to my step-sisters was from the sale of the house she shared with their father, which was then put into a college fund for them. Can you imagine how this knowledge could have changed my perception if I'd had it at the time? This is why money conversations are so important to have!

In my early college days, I recall having the courage to ask my dad about helping me pay for my college. It was a long time ago, but I remember him saying, "Your mother should be the one helping you. You made the decision to live with her (in 6th grade), so if anyone is going to help with your college, it should be her." Yep, that's how I remember it. So, basically my "Don't depend on anyone else" money message was solidified. I was on my own. Knowing that my mom couldn't help financially, if I wanted a degree, I needed to pay for it myself. I applied for scholarships, grants, financial aid and then started at a community college to keep costs down. I quickly switched to night school (5-10 p.m., 5 nights a week) so that I could work full-time during the day. I got a job at a print shop that paid $5.00/hr. I was making it happen!

About a year into my Associate's Degree studies, a teacher influenced me to go into industrial and organizational psychology. Professor Steve said, "There's a new field emerging, industrial and organizational psychology. That is where the money is, especially as a psychologist; if you are willing to be a consultant and travel a lot." Score! Travel is in my blood since my dad worked for the airlines! But, Steve said, "You will want the doctorate degree to make it, especially as a female in the consulting world." I took his advice and went for it.

When I began my bachelor's degree, I simultaneously started my own silk-screen business, *Koala-T Silkscreen*. I was good at art and graphics and I had learned a lot from my printing job. I was then fully immersed in school, still working full-time at a different print shop, and running my silk screen business late at night. I was truly burning the candle at both ends and I had the empty Mountain Dew cans to prove it! The business was very successful but I was exhausted. I paid off my cargo van, which I bought when my first car broke down, and, unknowingly at the time, would become my future home. When I finished my BA, I sold the business for $20,000 and that was my start-up funding for my Master's Degree and Ph.D. I am very proud to say I finished my MA in only a year.

About 8 years into my schooling my grandpa, the iron worker, asked me if I was "stupid" for taking so long to graduate college. He had no idea there were various levels or degrees and didn't realize that I was getting my doctorate. I wasn't offended. I thought it was comical and loved him for it. He was always so forthright with his thoughts.

What both parents offered me instead of tuition was a roof over my head (rent free as long as I was in school) and meals. For those who know me this is a big deal because as a farm girl, I could put anyone in the poorhouse with the amount of food that I could consume in a day; think *Man v. Food* reality show! I lived with my mom in Phoenix for the first three years of college, then back at the Minnesota farmhouse I grew up in (sans Dad and Step-mom) for another two years, and then for a brief stint at their California home when I started graduate school.

I did not attend any graduation ceremonies (AA, BA, MA) until I finished my doctorate—It was a tremendous accomplishment! In the end, I was broke and in debt. My last year of school, I temporarily moved into a friend's garage and then for a short time I lived in my van (yep, my cargo van) in front of another friend's house—this was before #Vanlife was cool! Looking back, my grandpa was right, I was stupid, because I was a young woman going to school in a suburb of Los Angeles, California; not the safest city in the world, and living in my van. Not long after hearing of my living arrangements, two classmates took me in by offering me a room in their basement, thank you Donna and Ken!

For food, I survived off happy hour buffets, which back then were free with a purchase of a $1 beer. And I also remember scrounging up 49 cents inside my car to buy a Taco Bell burrito—Ironic since I went to work for the company as my first job with my Ph.D. I have been to that destitute and hungry place, but I had purpose, a vision and my van; it was worth it. I had learned to survive in the unpredictable and unforgiveable jungle and some key money messages had already been imprinted into my DNA, "Never be dependent on anyone else for money, or a roof over your head!" Food is another story, though. My ex-husband would tell you I dated and married him because his refrigerator always had more food than mine (which was eternally empty); and unfortunately, he gained 100 pounds within the first few years being married by trying to keep up—oops.

For the record, my dad and step-mom did help me by covering the very last class of my 9-year education! With all sincerity, that meant a lot and helped me when I really needed it. Thank you!

*Money Message:* Where there is a will, there IS a way. Growing up in the United States, I was fortunate to live in a culture of opportunity, especially for women. I quickly learned that I could do anything once I set my mind to it. Over the years many people have called me "lucky." I bristle when I hear this, knowing what I sacrificed to get where I am today. One of my favorite sayings comes from the Roman philosopher Seneca, "Luck is where opportunity meets preparation!" This statement means a lot to me, simply stated, everyone plays a role in creating some of their own luck. I took this to heart. I prepared myself by going to school and working hard and then moved many times (cross country) when opportunities arose in order to advance my education and career.

And, a big "Thank You" to Professor Steve (who passed away shortly after giving me his advice), I did it!

*Amy's advice on college:* For those interested in embarking on a college degree who have concerns about the expense, here is my advice; take on as little debt as possible! Crazy advice, right? But get creative! If you're contemplating going to college and want to know how to finish with the least amount of debt, take the path of least resistance and minimize your debt to accomplish the goal. No matter what people tell you, in many cases – especially for undergrad - the school's name is not as important as you might think. Unless you're looking at attending an ivy league school, find a school that is affordable and offers degrees that you want, and the learning method that works for you. Americans are finding that schools in other countries can be significantly cheaper - like Canada. And virtual colleges are now mainstream. College name recognition may nor may not be important, even if you're going on to post-graduate degrees, but credentialing does matter, so do your homework.

Employ a strategy that includes grants, scholarships, and internships. My strategy in graduate school was selling my silk screen shop, quitting my job at the other print shop and going to work for the university instead as a Student Advisor. As a school employee I was entitled to two free classes per quarter. I was also then on the inside of the institution, which allowed me to expedite my dissertation process because I had more frequent access to my professors. I didn't make going to school a career. In the end, I ended up with a $100,000 degree and only $20,000 in student loan debt—which took me ten years to pay off. Don't stay on campus unless housing is cheaper or a part of your work-study (E.g., Resident Assistant). Be smart about your education and financial choices!

## Park Gift Shop

When I was 18, unknowingly, my mom gave me the biggest money lesson of my life. I was working at my first print shop job and attending night school. One day my car broke down. When the repair was finished the mechanic informed me that the cost to get my car back would be $328. I went home and told my mom that my car was ready and that I needed $328. I will never forget her reply, "Welcome to the adult world, kid!"

She never wavered; not kidding. I had to ride my bike to work at 6 a.m. and then across town to college for three weeks until my $5/hour job would cover the repair costs. To prevent being stranded from happening again, I traded that broken down car for a new cargo van; $320 a month for 5 years (60 payments in total), yes, that van!

I learned the definition of "savings account" and "emergency funds" all in that week. But knowing and doing are two different things. Even knowing the importance of having some emergency funds, by the end of my college years, I had no savings or emergency funds left to my name. But as soon as I was able to start my professional career, it became a priority. I tell people now to save! Even if it is a few dollars a week or a little into a 401K, find a way to set it aside. You'll be glad you did.

Another flashback scene in my movie would be when I learned the difference between a need and a want. One weekend while in graduate school my friends from Minnesota came to visit me in Los Angeles. We decided to take the van on a road trip to Ensenada, Mexico, through Tijuana. While we were shopping around, I fell in love with this beautiful long, super-soft, black leather jacket. It was $300! I told myself, "No, you NEED to purchase books for your next semester of school." Hours later, I could not get that stupid coat out of my head, yet I knew the consequences. I WANTED it so bad. Guess what I did? Yep, bought it!

Fortunately, a classmate loaned me her books so that I could study for the exams. Thank you! I passed the class. I never purchased the books and I still have that coat.

Jumping to another quick Park Gift Shop movie scene; everyone should pay attention to this one! I was having a conversation with the finance manager, Joe, at the casino where I worked. Joe was able to retire at a young age and was working for fun. A novel concept for me. One day I asked him his secret. He replied, "Paying cash for large purchases vs credit. If you save up to buy a car and it takes you many years, when you go to make that purchase you spend less. Here's why. When you use credit, that extra $1600 upgrade for leather seats is only $50 a month–sounds great so you do it. But if you pay cash, you quickly realize that you can live without those leather seats and you can keep $1600 of your hard-earned money in the bank." This two-minute conversation with

Joe transformed my financial life! It took several years to get out from under the $60,000 in personal debt my ex-husband and I had accrued together. Since then, I pay cash for things as often as possible (or use a credit card but ALWAYS pay off the monthly balance in full).

A proud financial moment occurred about 18 years ago when Cindy and I wrote a $35,000 check for a used Mastercraft waterski boat. We called the boat *Cinful*; first because it was Cindy's nickname, and second, because for me it was a sinful financial purchase. Decades later, I made Joe's advice my reality. "Thanks, Joe!"

*Money Message:* The lesson from my mom continued to build on my already deeply forming money message theme: Never trust anybody to be my source of income. I needed to be financially independent. And, regarding that coat that I bought and eventually the boat–I have a saying: "The meaning of life is choices."

## Currency River

On a vacation to Germany, I wanted to buy an expensive pair of hiking boots; made with one continuous piece of high-grade leather and only available in Germany (apparently, I have a thing for leather, including leather shoes!) Earlier that day I unknowingly lost my credit card. I asked my then husband to borrow his so that I could make this purchase and he said, 'no!' I begged him. He said, "no!" He didn't believe that I *needed* another pair of hiking boots (this transference being *his* childhood money message of scarcity, mixed with his Baby Boomer belief that the man of the house controls the money). I was livid! Having freedom as my personal value and a money message that "If I'm contributing to the household income, I have some discretion on how the money can be spent." The boots did not get purchased. We ended up arguing about this situation for months, then years. We went to counseling and ultimately, we divorced. Over the boots you may ask? No, but that was the indicator that I was not with someone with mutual values, and it was the catalyst that marked the beginning of the end.

Looking back, my and my ex-husband's money messages varied greatly and were influenced by many competing factors over our life together. We differed in our money mindsets (spender vs saver), gender (female vs male) and generation (Gen Xer vs Boomer), and none of our money messages associated with these differences were ever explored or discussed, not even during counseling. How does this story fit into the money roles? In my lifetime, I have played each of the roles: victim, follower, provider, controller and partner...

*Money Message:* I have always believed that in a relationship, when you start with approximately equal net worth, your financial management should be combined and managed using the Partnership role. Even if you have separate spending, giving and investment accounts, the management and knowledge of the whole picture is what I am referring to here. Therefore, I believe in putting in the effort to be Partners on the money bridge. In my world now, Cindy and I work hard to make sure that both of us *know how* to manage and access our financial accounts, *where* everything is located, *who* to contact in case of an emergency, *what* is available and more importantly what is not available (a budget), and *when* things need to happen (pay taxes). Both of us have a clear understanding of what is required to keep things moving seamlessly. While we do each have our preferred lanes when it comes to financial responsibilities, we both *can* do what needs to be done. We never want to be taken off guard financially if or when life falls... And today, I own at least 10 pairs of hiking boots, including an exact duplicate of that German pair. In hindsight, maybe it is a good thing that I didn't purchase those really cool looking hiking boots back then, I would have worn them with my business suits!

### Life Falls

A life falls event that was a pivotal part of my life and created many of my personal mottos was the loss of my sister Tammy. As a high school senior, at age 17, Tammy was killed in a car accident by a drunk driver. I was 15. The loss forever changed my life and that of my sisters and our parents.

*Money Message:* Because of this single tragic moment in time, a money message that I live by today is: Live today as if there is no tomorrow, but plan for tomorrow in case there is one! We all know that it's not *if,* but rather *when* something will happen that rocks your world and requires you to make difficult choices and decisions. My insight here is to prepare and educate yourself in areas where you can so that when something happens, you are more prepared and knowledgeable to take care of the tactical side; which, in turn, should free you up to spend more time on the emotional aspects of the situation when needed–like grieving. Love you Angel Sister!

## Tall Tales Campground

Of all the stupid things that I did related to money, the two decisions that I *don't* regret making is buying a 3-wheeler with my scholarship money— back then they gave you cash and the lump sum allowed me to pay cash for the ATV, saving me a lot of interest, and I still paid my tuition. I didn't share the ATV part of my money-movie, but I'd be happy to someday if you ask me about it. The second decision was spending my college book money on that beautiful leather coat!

What I do regret is stealing those 10 tubes of Bonny Bell lip balm when I was six years old! Maybe I should have just taken one instead of 10 so I didn't feel compelled to share one with my sister who in turn, snitched on me to dad; which resulted in me groveling in front of the Target store manager, scaring the crap out of me!

*Money Messages:* (1) Sometimes you gotta give into the WANT! Even if you're going to have to make up the difference later; (2) Stealing is wrong!

## Shooting Stars

Here is my interview on the Today Show:

**Your Courageous Money movie is a masterpiece. Where did you get the great stories for each of the scenes?**

These were real snippets of my life, and as with everyone's story, you can't make this stuff up!

**What was your favorite or most memorable scene?**

Scrounging for change in my car to buy a taco bell burrito! And, buying that ATV with my scholarship money.

**If you openly shared different perspectives of the same scene with someone, do you have new insights?**

Yes! I shared many of these stories with my dad and step-mom and then listened to their perspectives of the same events. It freed me from a life-time of assumptions and not knowing the whole story.

**What was your favorite twist or turn in the movie?**

Coming out as gay and still having a successful career.

**What was your favorite triumph or overcoming a challenge scene?**

Working full-time and going to school full-time for 9 years to pay for my doctorate degree. That was a labor of love and I thank Professor Steve for providing the encouragement and direction at the right time in my life.

**Just curious, did you notice a theme of food, the relationship with food, or the consumption of food surface in your movie scenes? What connections between food and money are true for you?**

Yes! There is definitely a greater connection between food and money that we did not explore in this book. Maybe our next book should be your adventure through the buffet line. My connection is all about how I consume both money and food. I like big, hearty, satiating, real meals, not snack food. My family on both sides has always been known for our massive quantity eating abilities. I've been well-known throughout out my life as the "skinny-bitch" who can consume unimaginable amounts of food at one sitting. My sister and I take pride in this freakish ability (even though we shouldn't). Cindy's dad found our eating capacities to be a spectator's sport. One time at the end of a large meal he offered to buy me a banana split at Dairy Queen to see if I could eat it. I replied, "Duh, let's go! Ice cream is easy, it melts in between what has already been eaten." And he never stopped talking about the all-you-can eat steak night in Cancun with my sister! In addition to the side dishes, I ate 4 filets and she ate 5. You go girl!

I spend money the same way I eat; big and bold! I hate buying little things, like knickknacks, ice-cream cones, or electronic accessories, but I like buying big ticket items. As Cindy put it one time, "You won't buy yourself a new phone case for $10, when the old one is so scratched that you can't see the keyboard, but you have no problem buying outdoor gear, an ATV, a new bike or even a new house!"

And, it doesn't have to be NEW! Another similarity between food and money is that I'm cheap – I don't need to have a new meal each day (I can eat left-overs for days) and I don't need to buy everything new (I buy used cars, tools, gear, etc.).

**If money were a person sitting next to me at the dinner table, what conversation would I have with money?**

My conversation with money is simple, "Money, I just wanted to say thank you for all of the experiences that you have given me, all of the opportunities to travel and spend time with family and friends over the years, and please don't leave me at any time because I love you!"

Money replies, "Then, don't be stupid!"

# Cindy's Adventure Movie Through Money National Park

*"Well behaved women rarely make history." ~Attributed to Many*

### Park Entrance Fee

The three words that I think of when I hear the word money are: Vital. Complex. Independence.

### Money Mindset Mine

Unlike many who will have one Money Mindset high on the list, my temperament would suggest I'm all four Money Mindsets equally, because in most assessments I'm a chameleon. Add to that I'm a Gemini, so there are 8 types for me—The Good 4 and the Evil 4! There is an up and downside to this configuration. I am a Jill of all trades and master of many. While this makes me highly adaptable and a strong leader, I can also be very hard to pin down at any given moment, and people aren't always certain which version of me they are getting... Ever see the Disney movie InsideOut? That's my brain—24/7! Ironically, that was also the name I chose for my Organizational Development Firm (InsideOut Discovery), long before that movie was conceived! It wasn't always the case, but today, I embrace being "the divergent."

Here's how I relate to each of the four money mindsets:

**Saver:** I'm surprisingly good at delayed gratification. I can save up for something that I want and I can even wait to get it until it goes on sale. I have been known to have great willpower.

I also have some very early memories of my mom and grandmother taking me to the bank. The former to deposit small amounts from gifts or allowance into my savings account, as she did the same into to the family "Christmas Club" account; and the latter to make deposits for the Boat Shop she owned with my grandfather. I recall meeting and shaking bankers' hands—maybe this explains why part of my career was spent working at a bank! All of the excitement was usually followed by a reward of lunch out with Grandma! Saving money = positive memories and GOOD FOOD! Up until the Covid-19 pandemic, business meetings over lunch were always my favorite! And while my family was pretty much middle-class, looking back, I think there may have been some level of elevated status that I associated with those events.

**Spender:** If I really want something, I am often willing to splurge on it, even if it means I have to sacrifice later. When I was a kid and given money for candy, I would spend it ALL and then eat all of the candy just as fast! Usually resulting in an upset tummy. No surprise I'm not a big sugar fiend, today. The other "spender" quality that I claim is that I love to spend money on other people—often more so than myself. I also like to spend money on good food—not necessarily fancy food (although that's fun sometimes), but spending money on good food *for* other people (either food I cook or at a restaurant), well that's like a drug for me! Some of my favorite charities are centered around feeding people. It's funny how much food seems to be tied to my money messages! I may have gotten this from my dad, who was also a connoisseur of food, he too loved to "treat" others.

**Investor:** I can be a risk-taker especially if I have a "feeling" about something like an investment, I go for it. In general, I have very good intuition and sometimes I use that as part of my investment strategy (watch all the financial planners cringe now). I've always been ahead of my time especially when it comes to technology and trends. I bought stock in RFID and Synthetic Blood in the early 2000s—long before the mainstream knew this tech existed... And lost my arse! If I'd have waited 10 years to invest in the same technologies, I'd be rolling in profit today. I was right about the technology; it just took longer for the rest of the world to come around.

While I have been known to invest in things that have "potential" to be huge, I've also made some very wise investment decisions on much more than gut feeling—Apple stock, for one. I may start with intuition, but then I do the homework. Sometimes the level of research I conduct can be mind-numbing, even to me! I see all the gray areas and I like to run down all the possible scenarios and outcomes. I've invested in quite a few things over the years. Some paid off, some didn't, but money is fluid (currency), and you can always make more, right? So, I have to be willing to go with the flow.

There have been a few occasions when I've been frustrated because I let someone else (often a financial advisor) convince me to sell something that I intuitively knew I shouldn't sell. Netflix stock is a great example. I bought Netflix in the early 2000s when the DVD-by-mail business was booming, but I also saw the signs of them moving into the digital age. The stock was quite volatile and for a few years and I had a planner that pushed me constantly to sell it. I finally gave in. To this day, I regret the decision, so I recently bought more. The lesson for me was that there will be times I should listen to the expert, but sometimes, I also should listen to the expert inside.

**Giver:** I like to give more than receive. Don't get me wrong, a thoughtful gift received is always appreciated, and I come from a family that excels in thoughtful gift giving! Still, if money were no object, I'd regularly give gifts to people just for the fun of it. In terms of philanthropy, I'm often more inclined to write a check than to show up with a hammer and nails; and this allows me to support multiple charities. I like to spread it around. When it comes to the empathy and intuition side of Giver, I have that in spades, too—My co-author's father has described me as having "scary intuition."—Another double-edged sword, for which I sometimes have to protect my own energy. It's one of the reasons I turned to coaching as a leadership skill early in my career vs. instructor, mentor and manager roles—all of which are discussed in our books *Coaching for Commitment, 3ʳᵈ Ed.* And *Coaching for Commitment Simplified.* Coaching allows me to remain neutral and be a sounding board and a mirror, not the person responsible for someone else's outcomes; thereby protecting my own energy in the process of letting someone else have the satisfaction of using their own wisdom and being their own expert. In my mind, it's another form of giving.

*Money Message:* As a result of my multi-faceted money mindset nature, one might wonder how I could possibly refine this down to just a few money messages? The committee in my head agrees there are three main insights from my multitude of Money Mindsets: (1) I have the ability to see money for what it is and for what it can be/do; (2) I have the adaptability to apply the right mindset at the right time, and if I miscalculate, I also have the inherent flexibility to change course; (3) I can use money (instead of money using me) to manifest whatever I choose/need and desire—I am fluid and so is money; which means I can always find a way to make more. No surprise here, there may be a 4th underlying message, (4) While I'm truly not obsessed with it, it seems food is somehow tied to success or prosperity in my minds-eye. One last quick example: When I went off to college, I wanted to be a star on Broadway. After a vocal-chord surgery at age 19 left me re-considering my options (I recovered fully), I eventually decided that I didn't want to starve for my craft. So, I changed my major to Communications and left Broadway behind. True story! I would willingly go without many other things before I'd starve.

## Fountain of Youth

I grew up in the 70s and 80s in a middle-class household in a largely blue-collar, conservative-leaning small town in Ohio, in a typical nuclear family with two parents and a sister who is four years older. My mom was a stay-at-home Mom whom I remember reading to us, driving us to dance lessons, swimming lessons, a never-ending slew of some kind of lessons. She did our laundry, made us clothes, packed our lunches and cooked our meals. She worked HARD! She taught us manners and made us cookies—I may have complained about washing dishes at my house, but when staying with a friend I darn well knew I'd better offer to help out! My mom is well-liked by pretty much everyone she meets and she set an example for us. She has a smile that lights a room. One thing she taught me that I treasure more than anything, is how to enjoy my own company—I'm not sure exactly how she passed on the independent streak that my sister and I both have, but I'm so grateful she did. I like myself enough to spend time alone! I am never bored when I'm alone because I am comfortable being my own best friend. What an asset! Thanks Mom!

The women in my family don't sit still. My mom, sis and grandma, all the same. Always doing something: A project, gardening, crafting, etc. I am more prone to sitting still then they, but I still always have too many balls in the air! My grandma worked into her 80s even after being diagnosed with Dementia, and my father also worked to the end of his life on this planet; he was in his early 70s. Work and productivity are important in my family.

When I was young it seemed like my dad worked a lot. Sometimes two jobs. Dad drove the old Gremlin to work, while Mom drove the Plymouth and later the Buick. Today, I realize that most everyone in Ohio back then had a "rust bucket," but looking back, I wonder if that made me think we were financially struggling. I know now after having conversations with my sister, we were fine. My dad liked to work and he had such a strong work ethic, sense of responsibility and desire to take care of his family, he did what he did out of love and because truly, I think work was his love, his hobby and his escape from a houseful of women and two female dogs!

My dad was a giving man who was not afraid to dream. He instilled that in me. Thanks Daddy! And, I joked with my sister recently that of all the great traits we could have inherited from our dad, we both got the "workaholic" gene. I run multiple businesses and sometimes I wonder if she, like my dad, will ever retire. Looking back, I think my dad was also in a constant pursuit of more—in part because he was raised poor—he wanted more for himself and for us. We lost him in 2017, too young, too soon and in a traumatic way that had an impact. I know he is always with me and yet the lack of his physical presence is something I will never get used to. I wish I had indulged his advice giving more—He loved to supervise! He is still managing, just from a different place. I am always and still wanting to make him proud and yet; I wonder what part stress, drive and the pursuit of more played into his shortened longevity and co-morbidities. He chose work and financial security over health—so, even as I tell myself to be present and to get up and do that workout after being in front of a computer all day, and that my health is more important than anything; my terrible work habits and growing to-do list are hard to set aside. Because like Dad, I always want the satisfaction that comes from earning and succeeding professionally. Family systems (patterns passed down from generation to generation) are hard to escape!

In my recollection, Dad and Mom made us feel like we could be anything—our going to college was never discussed but always assumed—so we went. While at the time I remember hearing phrases like "you need something to fall back on."

In my teenage head, I always assumed that was because: (1) They were trying to protect us based on the assumption that both of us would have traditional marriages and kids and maybe have to work due to some marital failure, or (2) They didn't want to be financially responsible for their adult children, like so many parents are today. Either way, we both went to college! So good job, Mom and Dad!

One more story here because I can't help myself. I played softball on a winning community league team from about age 12-16. My last year playing ball, my dad and I made a bet. If I hit a homerun that season, he would buy me a Moped. I spent the whole season trying for that homerun! That was my first mistake, I was trying too hard. The last game of the season, I hit two triples in a row and had one of the best games in my career. My dad was really proud of me, so after the game I confidently asked him if I could have the moped since, "Two triples have to be as good as a homerun!" Dad said, "No." First, I'm relatively certain that my dad was thanking his lucky stars my triples did not turn into homeruns that day! Second, what I learned is that sometimes there is no negotiation. A bet is a bet and no matter how well you do, a triple is not a homerun. I survived.

*Money Message:* The money messages and insights I adopted in my formative years are: (1) I can do it MYSELF (our family motto)! You have to be able to take care of yourself financially and otherwise. You can't fully rely on someone else to do it for you. The consequences of not being financially independent could also mean not having freedom of choice, such as leaving a bad marriage; (2) Anything worth doing is worth doing right, which means we give more than 100% to everything we do and sometimes we are hard on ourselves, too prone to looking at all the things that aren't "good enough" vs. looking at the awesomeness of what we have accomplished. Clearly there are no perfectionists in *my* family! (3) Don't sit still—Sitting still = Lazy and; (4) We take care of family. (5) Always do your best, even if you don't get the moped!

If I were to rewrite any messages they would be: Changing "I can do it myself," to when I can't do it myself, I should be better at asking for help. And, that sometimes, being still for a while can ultimately make you more creative and productive!

# COURAGEOUS MONEY: YOUR ADVENTURE THROUGH MONEY NATIONAL PARK

## Gender Mountain

I was a gregarious, loving and very talkative child! Back then the words "*little girls are meant to be seen and not heard*" beat a regular rhythm in my head!" Did I mention my grandparents were from the silent generation and my parents were on the cusp? Oh, and my sister was the quiet one. Thankfully today, I know I listen as much as I talk, especially when I'm coaching; but back then, "You talk too much," was a common refrain from teachers, family and probably strangers! I can remember my Uncle Bob promising me a nickel for every minute I could stay silent—not a high-earning prospect for me. I often wonder, would it have been different if I had been a boy? Boys were expected to be talkative and ask questions and demand to be heard. No matter, I got the last word! Because talking became a cornerstone of my professional life. Talking *a lot,* it turns out, can be a great way of making a living!!

Growing up, I played softball, danced, swam and dived competitively, starred in high school musicals and played in the band. I had a very diverse and active upbringing. I don't remember hearing "you can't, you're a girl," but then again, I wasn't trying to wrestle or be on the football team. I volunteered as a candy striper one year and I do remember people pushing me to go into nursing after that (nursing and teacher were "good" career choices for girls back in the 80s), but I honestly believe that was more about my ability to be a compassionate caregiver, clean up vomit without vomiting myself, and see blood without fainting. Alas I was terrible at math, so that was a non-sequitur.

I really have to give my parents credit. I believe they instilled in my sister and me that we could be anything we wanted to be career-wise. I don't remember them ever telling us we couldn't pursue a certain career because we were girls. I obviously took that to heart because I still think I can do anything I put my mind to! Gender be damned.

I had some good female role models. Even in college in Texas, there were more female professors than one would have thought possible back then. I did have one male history professor who was about 100 years old, smoked cigars in class, and liked for the young "pretty" girls to visit his office to rewrite test questions to "improve our grades..." Let's just assume he wasn't looking at our boobs the entire time...

Despite that, being treated "like a girl" probably became much more apparent to me when I entered the work force in earnest. I say to the young women I coach today that things were different back then. Doesn't make it right, but they were. We put up with things that we shouldn't have because "it was the way it was," and because on some level I guess we believed we had to. Women were also told back then to "use what you have," a nice butt, big breasts, etcetera to get ahead. To be clear, I'm NOT talking about sex; I'm talking about "feminine wiles." Which of course is a trap, because when someone hits on you in earnest then you have no recourse, because you obviously "brought it on yourself." If I could include an eye-roll emoji here I would! Can I just say a big thank you to all the young women (and the not so young ones) who are now setting a better example for women in the workplace.

In my professional history, I had a couple of great female bosses whom I learned a lot from. I was also talked down to, dismissed, flirted with and ogled by men I've worked for, which today would easily be considered harassment. I, like many women my age, was always careful of how I presented myself for obvious reasons. How does that relate to Money? I've likely been fired once and denied raises and promotions because I was a woman vs. a man. I was at times strong, outspoken and direct when that was not expected or appreciated by men I worked with; and yet I still managed to get a few promotions for the same reasons. I'd be lying if I said going to work for myself wasn't a huge relief from corporate posturing. In the end, right or wrong gender does play a part in who we are, what we earn and how we see ourselves, especially at work.

Lesbian or not, prior to the last few years I am not certain I would have labeled myself as a feminist. Now, I probably would. I think it's important that women have equal rights, equal opportunities and equal pay to men. I think that if women do the work, they should be compensated for it. I think they have the right not to be harassed. If that makes me a feminist. I can live with that. I am also a firm believer in women supporting women. Throwing another woman to the wolves just to get ahead professionally (especially if the wolf is male) will quite simply come back and bite you someday. Don't do it. Professional women need to stick together as much as possible.

The biggest and still the most challenging part about being a woman in the workforce is the lack of equity in pay. Women still make significantly less than men and women of color, even less.

Maybe that's why after 15 years in the workforce, I escaped corporate America to start my first business. I just wasn't up for the political pandering that was required to continue to rise up the corporate ladder. So, I took the escape hatch instead and made my own way, several ways in fact. I have never regretted my decision!

*Money Message:* (1) Regardless of my gender, I can be and do anything! (2) No one can stop me from succeeding; (3) Gender doesn't dictate my ability to make money or manage it effectively.

### Generation Trail

My upbringing was a bit unique I think, because my parents were born on the cusp year of the traditionalist generation (also known as the silent generation) and the boomer generation; and my sister was born on the cusp year of the boomer generation and generation X. While my feet are solidly planted in Gen X, born in 1968, there is no question I was influenced by the other generations in my family.

I always found it odd that people refer to Gen Xers as the lost or forgotten generation because I never felt that way. Specifically, I relate to two tenets of my generation. I believe in the "work hard, play harder" philosophy. I work to play, and I should play more! I also wholly embrace technology, it's benefits, conveniences and even its challenges! For example, I have been working from home and conducting business through virtual means for at least 20 years; and around the turn of the century (2000), my then team created the first company-wide on-line learning course (award winning) for one of America's top financial institutions, before most businesses had websites. What else would you expect from the first Atari and Nintendo junkies who had access to the first home PCs, VCRs and a Walkman?

While my drive and independence don't come from being a latch-key kid, the beauty of being Gen X is that I can do math on my electronic devices and I can also count back change without using a cash register (I had a lemonade stand)! I am part of a generation where money was not yet invisible and I've seen the progression to bitcoin. I have overdrawn a checking account (in college) because if you have checks you have money, right? And, I've been using Venmo since before it went mainstream.

Another characteristic of my generation is not only do I want to make money, I want others to make it, too! And yes, while I have not been loyal in my longevity to any one employer other than myself, I have always strived to make the place I've worked better for having been there. Why was I not loyal to one employer for 30 years? I was the granddaughter of entrepreneurs, I watched much older friends lose everything in the Enron scandal, my father, our family and friends were impacted by the closing of the steel mills and auto plants in Ohio and recessions in the 80s. I remember where I was when Challenger exploded—1986, senior year, sitting in world history when it lit up the TV screen we were watching. Our biology teacher, Mr. Williams had applied to be on board, Christa McAuliffe was on board instead. We were stunned to silence. I vaguely remember waiting in line for gas during the oil embargo of the 70s with my dad. As to influences from the other generations in my family, my grandfather fought in WWII and my grandmother was a child of the Depression. I've discussed the work ethic I inherited from my parents, and I clearly picked-up the hoarding gene from my Grandmother's passed down scarcity experience as a child of the depression—although thankfully most of my hoarding is electronic and not really related to money—though I do have 25 years of stored data on my computer/cloud/hard drive and a 200k+ photo collection, so I guess there is a financial aspect to having a backup of the backup of the backup in the annual fees I pay for cloud storage!

If I may digress, the Covid-19 pandemic will be an interesting look into family systems in 20 years to see how this major life event changes the way we and future generations behave. Will it for instance, spike the prevalence of agoraphobia (fear of leaving the house), OCD (obsessive compulsive disorder) and germaphobia (fear of germs) among future generations who may not even remember the battle of the mask?

*Money Message:* My Money Message takeaways from this stop in Money National Park are: (1) We cannot escape our history, and even after careful consideration, it will continue to define us and our money behaviors, unless we choose and work to change them; (2) You have to be able to take care of yourself financially and otherwise—you can't fully rely on someone else to do it for you. Especially if tragedy strikes. (This theme also emerged for me in the Fountain of Youth section.); (3) I was privileged to be brought up in a time where technology was also evolving to the point of making life and money-making easier; E.g., online banking saved me from having to balance my checkbook!

## Culture Crater

I am mostly of white Anglo-Saxon Protestant decent. My surname Coe, is Welsh. My mom's maiden name was Schneider (German) and my grandmother's was King (English). One of the most interesting aspects of my heritage in my opinion is that I supposedly had a distant Aunt who sang for the Romanian Opera in the old days. While that part of my family comes from what was known then as "Austria-Hungary," we came to realize part of our roots might be in Transylvania, which I now say is why I am such a vampire who likes to stay up late and sleep in! I do my best work at night.

Speaking of cultures and culture shifts, when I went to college in Texas, everyone asked if I was related to David Alan Coe and I'd say, "Of course, he's my uncle!" (a lie) Because, you see, being a "damn Yankee" in Texas in the 80's was cause for immediate expulsion! Who knows though, I might be related to Sebastian Coe, the Welsh Olympian?

Growing up, we went to the local Lutheran church on Sunday's, except in the summers where instead we spent every weekend playing on the water at the Allegheny River in our neighboring state of Pennsylvania—a family tradition since my mom's childhood. My family was very involved in the church. We went to Sunday School, mom and I both sang in the choir (I was the youngest choir member), Mom and Dad both participated in church dinners, and Dad played on the church softball team and every week they wrote a check for the offering plate. Once in a while, if I tried to rebel from going to church, which I did in my teens, my attempts were often unsuccessful and ended with me crawling into the backseat of the car in a huff. Dad, maybe because he worked so much, liked for us to do things together as a family; especially church. I think my dad would have made a good Pastor and he probably secretly harbored that same thought.

During my formative years, I went through at least a four-year period where I was bullied regularly in Junior High. The bullying began in 5$^{th}$ grade by a teacher who had a difficult time adjusting to the fact that I was a very different temperament and learning style (read: ADHD before it was cool) from my older sister, whom she'd had as a student four years earlier. I was a bright kid who got bored easily, couldn't sit still, was highly distractable, and asked a lot of questions (teachers don't like that). That year, the kids just began mimicking the teacher's openly malignant comments and on it went through the 8$^{th}$ grade... My parents tried to intervene but those were different times. I thank my lucky stars that social media did not exist back then! I was a sensitive kid and the sting haunted me for years. It also served as a catalyst for my own personal brand of drive, ambition and unapologetically eclectic perspective on life; and it fueled my ambition to get out of that town one day and start over. The best revenge is a happy ending!

After leaving my hometown at 18 and heading to college at Sam Houston State University in Texas, I always said "Ohio was a great place to be from," and it was. While I still have family there and have a few long-lasting friendships from the years that I spent growing up there, I realized there was perhaps some jealously that I'd made it out and didn't return. There are many things that make much more sense to me now than they did then. For instance, why I never entirely fit into the culture of my hometown? I always dreamed of greater things and faraway places. To put it simply, I was a progressive, futuristic thinker in a conventional box who would never be satisfied with the status quo. What I know now is that while I consider myself to be moderately left of center in my views, my hometown was pretty darn conservative. Good people mostly, but many had not explored much beyond our county's borders and as a result their minds remained as closed as their passports. Leaving gave me wings.

Like so many towns in the Midwest the expectations are: You grow up, get married and have kids (hopefully in that order). While I dabbled in that kind of thinking in my "boy crazy" years, I think deep down I always knew that wouldn't be my path; it took a lot of years to find my true path. For instance, I had no idea I even liked girls until I was well into my 30s and as it turns out, only *one* girl, my spouse and co-author, Amy. Up until then I'd been married to a man and all of my past relationships were with the opposite sex. Talk about a culture-shift! Thankfully, I am blessed that my family was incredibly supportive, accepting and gracious. In case you can't relate, coming out to your family (when you didn't even know you were in the closet to start with) is *the* hardest part of being gay.

There are some pieces of this scene that I believe have crossover with Gender Mountain so in the spirit of brevity, I will address them there.

*Money Message:* You may be wondering how all of this culminates in a Money Message from this stop. Me too! Just kidding... (1) Money is a means of escape and freedom; (2) Money can take you where you want to go and help you become who you want to be; (3) Money can help you explore places that broaden your perspective; (4) Money pays for a quality education (and world-travel) that helps open your mind.

### Wildlife Viewing Area

Which park is my family? Bryce Canyon NP, Utah. Our favorite thing to do to our mom is to ask "Who's your favorite?" before giving her something we know she will love! Mom never answers this question – she just giggles!

My birth order: For the record, while I have many identifiable traits of the youngest child, there are enough years between my sister and I that I also have some traits of the oldest—my sense of responsibility being one of the most prolific.

Present Day: I adore my sister. She is one of the most generous of heart people I know. She bakes cookies for her neighbors and will literally give you her favorite thing if she thinks it means something to you. Over the years she has been there for me (and countless others) both emotionally and financially. She is the most thoughtful giver of gifts. She bought me a dress for my high school graduation with her hard-earned money from her summer job while she was in college—it was a big deal. Once when I was in my 20s on a teacher's salary, she gave me money for an apartment deposit so I could leave a bad relationship. She was with me when I bought my first car after college. As sisters go, she is the best! If I were picking my friends, she'd be at the top of the list! For sure she is the one I want on my side, always. Which is why our early relationship is the stuff of legend...

Picture it, 1968: Imagine being an only child for four years and then on your best birthday yet, your parents leave you with your grandmother and later bring home your present; a crying baby sister, who now shares your special day! Yep. TWINS! 4 years apart (we were born on the same day). Gemini Twins at that! (We have matching T-shirts that say "I can't remember if I'm supposed to be the good sister or the evil one!")

Let's just say that my being born didn't go over so well with the toddler version of my Sis. Add to that I was four years behind her in all things... I think she and her friends are cool, but they want nothing to do with this little pain in the butt. Thus, prompting me to behave more like a brat and tattling often—as if that was going to work; while secretly I'm crushed. I wish I'd known reverse psychology back then! I still feel bad about how much it pained my mom that we didn't get along. The only time I really knew my sister loved me in those days was when she wouldn't let *others* pick on me, even though she picked on me all the time. I now know this as some weird ritual rite of passage that exists among siblings.

Back then we could not have been more opposite. I was a blonde and bratty (her word), plus a bit of an actor who wanted to be the center of attention. LOOK! AT! ME! As the youngest child, I also was daring enough to push the boundaries with our parents, which I sometimes got away with. The fact that I got away with some things did not go over well, because my Sis was the dark-haired, serious, quiet-ish one, who did as she was told and didn't challenge the status quo. By rights, she should have been rewarded for good behavior, but instead I was distracting our parents and exhausting them into submission to get my way. Case and point I came home every day for a month in 7$^{th}$ grade wearing someone else's makeup until my mom finally gave in. My sister couldn't even wear mascara until high school!

Opposites in this case did not attract. Many years later we realized *we* should have been smarter and joined forces against our parents instead of each other, but alas, we were young and not child prodigies in strategic warfare. So, we fought each other instead...

Long story short, it took until she went off to college for us to get closer. Absence does make the heart grow fonder apparently, because now in our 50s and half a country away from one another, there isn't a thing we wouldn't do for each other. I'm often surprised by how much we really *are* alike and how much she's influenced my thinking. But back then. No way!

When it comes to money, I am so grateful that my sister and I don't have greed to contend with. We are also really good about sharing family responsibilities. We both feel a strong sense of familial commitment that has helped us be there for each other and our parents. We worked very well together when my father had his health crises, each taking our turn to help, and we each have our strengths. I appreciate this so much because I know it isn't the case with other families, where often one sibling takes on more than the others. We make a good team.

*Money Message:* My money messages here are: (1) The value of family is in relationships not money; (2) It's our responsibility to help take care of family should they need us. (3) A good family is a gift.

### The Park Gift Shop

Over the years, being a part of a partnership and not the higher wage earner in our household, I have contributed to our finances in various ways. While I continue to work for money, I admit I have a weird mental thing about having "my own" money to spend. The money I make working I feel should go to the "our" pot (not just the "mine" pot). So, I always have mad-money or a "cash stash" as I like to call it; a little cash (paper or virtual) that I have earned from a little side jobs, which I allow myself to use on frivolous things I like. Guilty pleasures like trips to the rock shop, books, a lunch out by myself, or buying a gift for someone just because. This is money that isn't budgeted or earmarked for some other purpose and is inconsequential to the family coffers. It's not that I can't do these things with "our" money, it's just that I like how it feels when I do them with "my" money. Money has crazy power over people! I come by this trait honestly because every woman in my family from my grandma down to me has had a cash stash. Some stashes are secret, some not. My dad used to joke that he'd hand over bigger bills to pay a merchant so that my mom could take the change to put in her stash! My Grandma always had a $50 tucked away in her wallet. My sister, who *is* the primary breadwinner in her house has one too! We Coe girls like to have money of *our own*!

When I left corporate America, I did so to start my own business. While doing so is always a brave pursuit, it was made easier by the fact that Amy had a good job with benefits that we could share (even though back then they came out of her paycheck after-tax, an inequity we lived with until the laws changed in 2008). That said, I have since started several businesses. The original business, InsideOut Discovery, my organizational development firm established in 2002, continues to be a constant. It is also the one that qualifies me for this writing.

I love the innovation that comes with creating diverse opportunities to make money. My entrepreneurship and experience in training/education, communications, marketing and technology have led me to own a popular food and travel blog (there's the "food" word again), an "INTERtainment" company, a digital storytelling/web design and social media consulting company, and an over fifty influencer site; almost all of which operate simultaneously and all in the pursuit of innovation, freedom and independent money-making!

As a kid, I used to invent things and imagine selling and making money from them—one time I made an "electric" toothbrush from a Kleenex box and my mouth sounds were the motor. I put up lemonade stands in the summers to make money. Sometimes Mom used to let us sell vegetables from her garden.

# COURAGEOUS MONEY: YOUR ADVENTURE THROUGH MONEY NATIONAL PARK

For a few years I was the top sales person of Girl Scout cookies in my troop, after canvasing the neighborhood and knocking on every door (my dad helped too because he'd take the order form to work). My poor Mom would then have to drive to every house that I got to on foot to help me drop them off. She deserved a medal! I don't know if I loved the sale, the connecting, being the center of attention or the earning (even when the money didn't go to me. I did get a trophy.) Maybe I liked all of it! To this day, I network in spite of myself! Now, at 52, I'm over feeling important and just want to figure out how to retire sooner!

Growing up, I don't remember earning a regular allowance. The tooth fairy came with quarters and 50-cent pieces, and our parents gave us money for things like good report cards. Of course, this did not benefit me much, as I was not a straight A student. I would have made more pulling out all my teeth! My sense is my parents dabbled with the allowance idea once or twice but I don't think it stuck - $5 a week stands out in my head? I do recall that every weekend when we went to "the river," we each got $1 to spend at the general store (back then there was penny candy). Every week, my sister would get the same paper bag of 100 Swedish fish - counted out meticulously by her hand (she still loves them), and I conversely would see how many different things I could get for my $1. Sometimes I'm sure the clerk's patience wore thin as they helped me count out how many Sixlets I could get for .20 cents, or how many mini-Sugar Daddy pops for .30 cents, etc. until I spent the whole dollar.

At age 16, I got my first job as a lifeguard and swim instructor because once again, I liked the idea of having my own money. Since I was on the swimming and diving teams, it was a convenient job because I was always at the pool. We had a family car, so I didn't have to spend my money on insurance or car payments. I don't recall ever pining for my own car.

I worked part-time throughout college so I could have some spending money outside of the money my parents gave me to support my living expenses. Then, I worked more so I could help supplement my moving off-campus into an apartment without roommates. I had a few different jobs during that time. I was a lifeguard, a data entry person, a public relations assistant and even a swim team coach. I always had a drive to work because I didn't like being broke, and if I'm honest, I think it made me feel important and capable. When I was a lifeguard on campus, that was a coveted position. We earned .25 more an hour than other minimum wage workers because we had to be certified and were considered "professionals." I loved that! Back then, that was $3.75 an hour! In today's dollars, that's a little less than $7.50 an hour.

If you've read my entire movie to this point you will be shocked to know that my "treat" every paycheck for working so hard was to buy myself a fast-food meal! Holy cow, back to food. WHAT?!?

Suffice it to say I feel a strong sense of personal accomplishment at being able to earn money and in having skills and experience to offer that are worthy of a paycheck. I also love the feeling of paying things off! Student loans, my first car, my second car... I'm still on my third car! I also felt strongly that it was important for me to give back to my parents for having contributed so much to my college expenses, and so once I was able, I took on my student loan payments and threw in a few fun vacations with Mom and Dad over the years. It makes me feel good to be self-sufficient and have enough left to share.

*Money Message:* The money messages here are: (1) I feel strongly that it's important to find ways to give back to those who have helped me financially along the way; (2) Earning money makes you feel good and worthy; (3) Spending money also makes you feel good! (4) You can always find a way to make money.

### Currency River

Currency means a few different things to me. In my business life, currency has been both money and bartering (I regularly trade services with clients). Sometimes even recognition has been currency!

With my ex-husband, I handled the finances. With my current spouse, Amy, she handles most of our finances. Bottom line for me is that I feel *capable* of managing the money and finances.

In my personal life, currency is money, but because I am not the primary breadwinner in our household, I have found it is also other things, time being the biggest. Time spent setting up, maintaining, and troubleshooting all of our technology, creating, designing and managing our social media and websites and cooking are just a few examples.

What's important to me right now is that I am part in the decision-making around money and finances and I also want to make sure I know the what/where/who/how of our finances. If something happens to Amy, where do I find things like our life insurance and who do I contact if I need to get information on medical benefits (that come from her job), etc. In terms of the Money Bridge, Amy and I work toward the Partnership in the middle.

I have at different times in my life played all of the other roles. When single, I was always in charge of my money management; sometimes even when dating, instead of letting someone else pay I might insist so I could remain in control (Controller). I should have let them contribute because it set up a scenario where I then had to be the provider for people who should have at least been sharing the responsibility.

The worst mistake I made as a Provider was letting my college boyfriend charge his senior year tuition ($10,000) on my credit card, because he didn't have any other means to pay for it. Later when we broke up, guess who got stuck paying that $10,000 credit card bill?! It took me years to pay it off. I went from being a provider to a victim overnight!

*Money Message:* I have one real money message in this section. I am willing to be trusting when it comes to sharing money responsibility with a partner as long as I have a say in it.

### Life Falls

Like anyone, I've had my share of Life Falls events happen. From the list that we provide in the book, I can say that I've experienced almost all of those events at one time or another. These are a few of my most vivid examples:

The first time I lost a job I was "downsized." It was my first job out of college. Prior to it, I had a great job with a great boss for two years, but they couldn't afford to bring me on full-time after graduation. There was a recession starting in Texas at the time. So, when I landed the new job, I was thrilled. To make the job work, I had just moved to a new apartment in a bigger city and bought a new car which meant more expenses. The pay was good, so when a few short months later when I was let go, I was horrified! While I recognized early on that my boss and I didn't see eye to eye on everything, I never expected him to let me go. I worked for him and a team of salespeople so my job description seemed to get longer by the day, I was pulled in several directions and as a result I was working evenings. As an hourly employee I got paid overtime to do the work. It was great money, and no one ever said I couldn't get overtime so I thought I was fine. One day, I came to work and was told officially that the position (a marketing assistant) had been eliminated due to budget cuts, and human resources watched me pack my desk and escort me out of the building. I remember feeling like a criminal! I had absolutely no idea what to do next. I was a hard worker and I'd never lost a job! It was humiliating! "OMG! I am unemployed. I'm going to have to tell my parents. Unacceptable!" This was back in the time before the internet so I couldn't just Google "What to do when you lose your job?" This was so far back in the day that the idea of moving back in with your parents was like buying a ticket to Loserville! (Times have changed.) To be honest I don't know how I figured out to apply for unemployment, but that's what I did. Those days you had to show up and apply in person. That too was completely demoralizing for me. I felt like I was taking money I didn't earn or deserve. I realize now that was crazy thinking because that is what unemployment was for, and I give myself credit for being resourceful. That story ended with me going back to school to pick up my secondary education teaching credential so I would have "job insurance" in case I ever got in a situation like that again! I needed a backup plan!

Divorce. I married my ex-husband at 27, even when I knew I shouldn't have (a lot of us do that). I loved him, yes. But he was a professional alcoholic. In that life, I felt like my financial security was always hanging in precarious balance. I made a good living (our pay was about equal) and I knew I was fully capable of taking care of my own financial needs with or without him; but I was always unsettled thinking that if he did something under the influence it might cause a catastrophic financial event that neither of us could recover from. It was a constant source of stress coupled with his ever-intensifying addiction behaviors. I'd finally reached my limit. Divorce is never easy regardless of the circumstances. While ours was I am proud to say, relatively amicable, I still decided to seek counseling afterward so I didn't carry that baggage into my next relationship!

My food and travel blog: Now that I see the connections between my money messages and food it is truly no wonder that I started a food and travel blog! It is also no wonder I had such a hard time shutting it down when it had run its course. I was getting restless and I wanted something fun and new that I loved—I love cooking for relaxation and because I also love feeding other people and I'm kind of a geek, it seemed the perfect fit. Until it became a full-time job for two people but there was only me! I got into the space before it was saturated like it is now and it was awesome. I built a solid following and started making income within a couple of years, but I struggled with finding a web designer who could implement my vision and increase the profitability of the site. In fact, I hired two and lost $8,000 on one site that never came to fruition. Lesson learned. So, I set out to build my own site. Doing quadruple duty of being the recipe creator, blogger, web designer, publicist and then some, I was consumed by the blog. Amy complained I was never present and she was right. When my dad had a health crisis, I decided to take some time off to spend it with my family which was 100% the right thing to do. It helped me see that I couldn't continue at that pace. But as much as I knew it was the right thing to shut it down, it took me a full year to make it happen. In fact, that was several years ago and it was just this year I let the domain name expire for good (the YouTube channel is still up – you may recall I'm an electronic hoarder). Even though it was my decision (and the right one) I realize now that it was hard because that decision impacted my perception of independence, self-sufficiency, responsibility and here it is again, the attachment I make between food and prosperity—I felt like I was letting people (my followers) down. When one door closes another one opens: It led to the opening of a new business creating websites for others and consulting on social media.

*Money Message:* What money messages came from my Life Falls experiences? Sometimes you have to take charge and make choices to take care of yourself, even if they are uncomfortable!

## Tall Tales Campground

Once something is in writing it can incriminate you! I refuse to be incriminated. LOL! The truth is I've probably blocked out any of these stories I may have had as a method of self-preservation.

*Money Message:* In case you ever run for office or get famous, don't tell stories you don't want shared across the internet! (I used to want to be famous, now most days I just want a nap!)

## Shooting Stars

Here is my interview on the Today Show:

**Your Courageous Money movie is a masterpiece. Where did you get the great stories for each of the scenes?**

Throughout the course of writing this book, we have been in awe of how easily these money conversations have flowed from others once they feel comfortable, safe and encouraged to share. As evidence of how well this process works, I must admit that until I sat down to write my own Money Movie, I didn't realize some of these connections and money messages existed for me. Even as the authors we have been surprised by the power of our own questions.

**What was your favorite or most memorable scene?**

The scenes where I revisit my childhood experiences are fun for me to look back on. When I called my sister to tell her I was doing this book and said she would have to read my story and "approve" what I was saying about her, she began to tell her own money memory stories from our childhood, including one about our dad taking her to the bank. I love that sharing our stories gets other people to want to share theirs!

**If you openly shared different perspectives of the same scene with someone, do you have new insights?**

Yes! This is the story of my life! (If I could I would insert a laughing emoji here). I have often had a different perspective when it comes to topics especially in family discussions. Did I mention I am usually the divergent? While our money movies often do not match up—remember we said people often see the same scenes very differently—it's cool when they do! The example I shared of my sister and my dad going to the bank (similar to my memory of me and my mom and gram going to the bank) is one example of how our money memories are similar and fueled our messaging, drive and desire to be financially independent and secure.

**What was your favorite twist or turn in the movie?**

I have two. One is just the reinforcement of how much creativity and innovation are a part of my life. I am not a one-lane gal. I know this of course and as a result have always tried to embrace the term "serial entrepreneur" because it is not about sticking with something, it is about experiencing EVERYTHING—sometimes all at once!

My ah-ha moment when I saw how much food plays a part in my life and messaging and how much I see food tied to privilege... (More on this in the question below about food.)

**What was your favorite triumph or overcoming a challenge scene?**

I love the story about my first involuntary job loss experience. I think it was truly the day when I became an adult in the financial sense. I really had to figure out where my next meal was going to come from and how to pay my rent and car payment.

**Just curious, did you notice a theme of food, the relationship with food, or the consumption of food surface in your movie scenes? What connections between food and money are true for you?**

Yes! Based on all I've shared, it is clearly all about the FOOD with me! It might as well be currency! I am laughing out loud right now because I realized that back in my Food and Travel blog days it was just that. I used to have a tag line that said, "Will Work for Food," in order to attract sponsors, free meals, free cooking gadgets, samples, etc.!

Making nice meals, having a nice meal out, paying for a nice meal for someone else, conducting business meetings over meals; in fact, cooking is actually how I unwind and de-stress! There is nothing I love more than having the gift of time and a whole day of cooking and creating in the kitchen.

The shear luxury of being able to share food, savor each bite and buy almost any food I want—Whether it's splurging on organic dairy and vegetables, or a steak and a great bottle of wine, and wanting others to be able to have the same opportunity—and if they don't, helping them to experience it… Maybe it is all those dinner conversations from my childhood that included statements like, "There are children starving in (fill in the blank poor country)" An American parental guilt-trip meme common in the 70s and 80s, used as a method if getting kids to clean their plates. In my case, acorn squash – YUK!

Food should be an experience for all! Speaking of experiences, what Amy and I do is create experiences for people. Even this book was a means of doing that. The only thing we should have added (based on my new revelations) is that you should pack a picnic lunch before you go on this adventure! Just out of curiosity: *"What is your Picnic Basket?"*

**If money were a person sitting next to me at the dinner table, what conversation would I have with money?**

The dinner table part of this is very apropos… "Money, thank you. Thank you for always being there when I needed you and for not letting me down. Even in my early days when I stretched you as thin as I dared, thought I had more than I did or could only use you in small amounts to take care of those bigger price tags like student loans and credit card bills, you came through for me. I have trusted you will be there, even when maybe I shouldn't have. Thank you for sharing your optimism with me! You have been a stable force in my life, even when I felt tested. I know I am blessed and for that I am grateful every day. You taught me your value and that hard work, drive and innovation can make you multiply and make many things possible, from adventures to giving back. While you are not the center of the universe, you are certainly a big player. We are a team Money and you're stuck with me!"

## COURAGEOUS MONEY: YOUR ADVENTURE THROUGH MONEY NATIONAL PARK

Money would reply, "Hold on for the ride."

# End Notes

## Introduction: Courageous Money

Median Income[1]

Dena[2]. "He Sacrifices His Health in Order to Make Money." Live, Love, Simple. April 13, 2011.

Stieg[3], Cory. "From the 'perfect' salary to keeping up with the Joneses, here's how money really affects your happiness." CNBC Make It. May 26, 2020.

## PART I. DEMYSTIFYING MONEY MESSAGES

### Mountains of Money Messages

Gates, Melinda. The Power of Lift. New York, NY: Flatiron Books, April 23, 2019.

U.S. Wealth Management.[4] "Women and Investing: How Psychology Plays a Role."

1. https://www.census.gov/library/stories/2019/09/us-median-household-income-not-significantly-different-from-2017.html

2. https://livelovesimple.com/sacrifice-health-make-money/#_853ae90f0351324bd73ea615e6487517__4c761f170e016836ff84498202b99827__853ae90f0351324bd73ea615e6487517_text_43ec3e5dee6e706af7766fffea512721_The_0bcef9c45bd8a48eda1b26eb0c61c869_20Dalai_0bcef9c45bd8a48eda1b26eb0c61c869_20Lama_0bcef9c45bd8a48eda1b26eb0c61c869_2C_0bcef9c45bd8a48eda1b26eb0c61c869_20when_0bcef9c45bd8a48eda1b26eb0c61c869_20asked_c0cb5f0fcf239ab3d9c1fcd31fff1efc_money_0bcef9c45bd8a48eda1b26eb0c61c869_20to_0bcef9c45bd8a48eda1b26eb0c61c869_20recuperate_0bcef9c45bd8a48eda1b26eb0c61c869_20his_0bcef9c45bd8a48eda1b26eb0c61c869_20health

3. https://www.cnbc.com/2020/05/26/how-your-salary-and-the-way-you-spend-money-affect-your-happiness.html

4. https://www.usbank.com/wealth-management/financial-perspectives/women-and-money/women-and-investing-how-psychology-plays-a-role.html#_853ae90f0351324bd73ea615e6487517__4c761f170e016836ff84498202b99827__853ae90f0351324bd73ea615e6487517_text_43ec3e5dee6e706af7766fffea512721_Women_0bcef9c45bd8a48eda1b

## Money See, Money Do

Bartlett[5], Carol, LCSW. "Bowen Family Model." Insight for Change.

Lieberman[6], Stuart. "A transgenerational theory." Wiley Online Library/ Journal of Family Therapy. Volume 1, Issue 3, 1979.

## Understanding the Movie in Your Mind

Kimball[7], Miles Spencer. 'The Four Agreements' by Don Miguel Ruiz (with Janet Mills) and `The Fifth Agreement' by Don Miguel Ruiz and Don Jose Ruiz (with Janet Mills)." Confessions of a Supply-Side Liberal.

Ruiz, Don Miguel. The Four Agreements. 6 Books, Amber-Allen Publishing, Inc. July 10, 2018

## Money Confidence

Weissberger[8], Tali. "The Difference Between Self Confidence and Self Esteem." ADDA.org. September 7, 2020.

Health Place.[9] "The Difference Between Self-Esteem and Self-Worth." August 22, 2018.

## Till Death Do Us Part

26eb0c61c869_20also_0bcef9c45bd8a48eda1b26eb0c61c869_20show_0bcef9c45bd8a48eda1b26eb0c61
c869_20a_0bcef9c45bd8a48eda1b26eb0c61c869_20tendency_c0cb5f0fcf239ab3d9c1fcd31fff1efc_signifi
cant_0bcef9c45bd8a48eda1b26eb0c61c869_20amounts_0bcef9c45bd8a48eda1b26eb0c61c869_20of_0b
cef9c45bd8a48eda1b26eb0c61c869_20compound_0bcef9c45bd8a48eda1b26eb0c61c869_20interest

5. http://www.insightforchange.com/enneagram_bowen.html

6. https://doi.org/10.1046/j..1979.00506.x

7. https://blog.supplysideliberal.com/post/2020/4/12/the-four-agreements-by-don-miguel-ruiz-and-the-fifth-agreement-by-don-miguel-ruiz-don-jose-ruiz-and-janet-mills

8. https://add.org/self-confidence-vs-self-esteem/

9. https://www.healthyplace.com/blogs/buildingselfesteem/2018/8/the-difference-between-self-esteem-and-self-worth

Chatzky[10], Jean. "How Women Can Plan for Outliving Their Husbands." The Balance. March 14, 2019.

U.S. Bank[11]. "Survey Says Women Are Leaving Money and Influence on the Table." U.S. Bank via Business Wire. March 5, 2020.

**Finding Your Courage in Finance**

Cynthia Tremaroli, JD. Zoom Interview. February 14, 2021.

**Exercise Courage**

DiPietro[12], Debra. "5 Bold Exercises to Work Your Courage Muscle." *Success*. June 23, 2017.

**What Doesn't Touch on Money**

Somers, Moira. Zoom Interview. August 31, 2020.

*Advice That Sticks*. UK: Practical Inspiration Publishing, 2018.

**PART II. WELCOME TO YOUR REAL-LIFE ACTION-ADVENTURE MOVIE!**

**Fellow Explorers**

Denise Cauley. Zoom Interview. June 9, 2020.

Candi Cross. Zoom Interview. June 9, 2020.

---

10. https://www.thebalance.com/retirement-plan-for-women-outliving-husbands-4139845#_853ae90f0351324bd73ea615e6487517__4c761f170e016836ff84498202b99827__853ae90f03 51324bd73ea615e6487517_text_43ec3e5dee6e706af7766fffea512721_Some_0bcef9c45bd8a48eda1b26e b0c61c869_2080_0bcef9c45bd8a48eda1b26eb0c61c869_20percent_0bcef9c45bd8a48eda1b26eb0c61c8 69_20of_0bcef9c45bd8a48eda1b26eb0c61c869_20married_c0cb5f0fcf239ab3d9c1fcd31fff1efc_when_0b cef9c45bd8a48eda1b26eb0c61c869_20their_0bcef9c45bd8a48eda1b26eb0c61c869_20spouses_0bcef9c4 5bd8a48eda1b26eb0c61c869_20were_0bcef9c45bd8a48eda1b26eb0c61c869_20alive

11. https://www.businesswire.com/news/home/20200305005270/en/Survey-Says-Women-Are-Leaving-Money-and-Influence-On-the-Table

12. https://www.success.com/5-bold-exercises-to-work-your-courage-muscle/

Vin Lee. Written Response. July 1, 2020.

Myles Meyers. Zoom Interview. June 30, 2020.

Gina Snyder. Zoom Interview. June 9, 2020.

Matthew Tepoorten. Zoom Interview. June 9, 2020.

**Adventure #3: Gender Mountain**

National Women's Law Center[13]. "The Wage Gap: The Who, How, Why and What to Do." Fact Sheet. April 2016.

Power[14], Robin. "Ep 20: Moira Somers on tackling investor behavior." The Evidence-Based Investor podcast. November 29, 2018.

Roy[15], J. "Top 10 Engineering Degrees, Female, 2017-18." Engineering by the numbers. American Society for Engineering Education. 2019.

Matias[16], Dani. "New Report Says Women Will Soon Be Majority of College-Educated U.S. Workers." NPR.org. June 20, 2019.

Clover[17], Katherine. "5 Unexpected Gender Differences in Children's Clothing." Parent Co. January 27, 2017.

Target[18]. "What's in Store: Moving Away from Gender-based Signs." August 7, 2015.

**Adventure #4: Generation Trail**

---

13. https://nwlc.org/wp-content/uploads/2016/04/The-Wage-Gap-The-Who-How-Why-and-What-to-Do-1.pdf

14. https://podcast.app/the-evidence-based-investor-p178427/

15. https://research.swe.org/2016/08/degree-attainment/

16. https://www.npr.org/2019/06/20/734408574/new-report-says-college-educated-women-will-soon-make-up-majority-of-u-s-labor-f

17. https://www.parent.com/5-unexpected-gender-differences-in-childrens-clothing/

18. https://corporate.target.com/article/2015/08/gender-based-signs-corporate

Ryback[19], Ralph. "From Baby Boomers to Generation Z." *Psychology Today.* February 22, 2016.

**Adventure #5: Culture Crater**

Budget Direct[20]. "8 ways different cultures deal with cash." Budget Direct Blog. October 29, 2019.

**Adventure #6: Wildlife Viewing Area (Sibling Dynamics and Birth Order)**

U.S. National Parks Travel Guide[21]. US-Parks.com.

Devine[22], Renee. "Psychological Birth Order in Blended Families." Adler Grad School. 2017.

Lorenzi[23], Natalie. "What to Know About Older, Younger, and Middle Child Personalities." Parents.com. September 18, 2019.

Zupek[24], Rachel. "Can birth order determine your career?" CNN.com. October 22, 2008.

19. https://www.psychologytoday.com/us/blog/the-truisms-wellness/201602/baby-boomers-generation-z

20. https://www.budgetdirect.com.au/blog/8-ways-different-cultures-deal-with-cash.html

21. https://www.us-parks.com/

22. https://alfredadler.edu/library/masters/2017/
renee-devine#_853ae90f0351324bd73ea615e6487517__4c761f170e016836ff84498202b99827__853ae9
0f0351324bd73ea615e6487517_text_43ec3e5dee6e706af7766fffea512721_The_0bcef9c45bd8a48eda1b2
6eb0c61c869_20importance_0bcef9c45bd8a48eda1b26eb0c61c869_20of_0bcef9c45bd8a48eda1b26eb0c
61c869_20birth_0bcef9c45bd8a48eda1b26eb0c61c869_20order_c0cb5f0fcf239ab3d9c1fcd31fff1efc_of_
0bcef9c45bd8a48eda1b26eb0c61c869_20personality_0bcef9c45bd8a48eda1b26eb0c61c869_20in_0bcef
9c45bd8a48eda1b26eb0c61c869_20an_0bcef9c45bd8a48eda1b26eb0c61c869_20individual._6cff047854
f19ac2aa52aac51bf3af4a_text_43ec3e5dee6e706af7766fffea512721_Each_0bcef9c45bd8a48eda1b26eb0c
61c869_20group_0bcef9c45bd8a48eda1b26eb0c61c869_20of_0bcef9c45bd8a48eda1b26eb0c61c869_20
siblings_0bcef9c45bd8a48eda1b26eb0c61c869_20from_c0cb5f0fcf239ab3d9c1fcd31fff1efc_is_0bcef9c45
bd8a48eda1b26eb0c61c869_20described_0bcef9c45bd8a48eda1b26eb0c61c869_20as_0bcef9c45bd8a48
eda1b26eb0c61c869_20a_0bcef9c45bd8a48eda1b26eb0c61c869_20sibship

23. https://www.parents.com/baby/development/sibling-issues/how-birth-order-shapes-personality/

24. https://www.cnn.com/2008/LIVING/worklife/10/22/cb.birth.order.career/index.html

**Adventure #8: Currency River (The Partnership Bridge)**

Online Etymology Dictionary[25]. "current."

**Cindy's Adventure Movie Through Money National Park**

Coe, Cindy and Zehnder, Amy. Coaching for Commitment 3$^{rd}$ Ed., 2007

25. https://www.etymonline.com/word/current

# Meet the Authors

Cindy Coe and Amy Zehnder (a.k.a. CCnDoc) are unapologetically eclectic entrepreneurs and digital creators. Dubbed the "Dynamic Duo," their approach to storytelling, life, food, travel, business, money and relationships is only limited by their imaginations, which are unlimited! "Innovation is who we are, in fact it's one of our core values!"

Now living in the mountains of rural Southern Colorado and settling down a bit after 25 years of business travel and adventures, these two #Over50Influencers have more ideas than time.

As a corporate road-warrior for over 25 years, Amy (Doc) has helped hundreds of families, leaders and individuals enhance their communication and leadership effectiveness. She is widely known for her compelling vision, creative solutions, strategic thinking and inspiring leadership style. As a wealth psychologist, her work includes executive coaching, organizational development, executive and leadership development, succession planning, and family governance work focused on shared decision-making. Amy is highly credentialed with her Ph.D. in Industrial and organizational psychology, her Professional Coaching Certification (PCC) from the International Coach

Federation and the prestigious Certified Family Business Advisor (CFBA) designation from the Family Firm Institute's Global Education Network.

Cindy (CC), now semi-retired, is a self-dubbed "Simplification Engineer" who was once an award-winning learning and development leader, the CEO of a successful international organizational development firm, a sought-after executive coach, leadership development expert, keynote speaker as well as a popular blogger and the creator of more than one start-up.

These digital storytellers love creating experiences for others!

More titles by CCnDoc: *Coaching for Commitment Simplified, Courageous Money™: Your Adventure Through Money National Park™* and *The BIG Book of Southern Colorado Wildflowers: For kids of all ages.*

**CCnDoc can each be found on LinkedIn, or check out all of their adVentures on social media @CCnDoc and at www.CCnDoc.com[1].**

**For book club and press virtual appearances, visit the Courageous Money website at www.MoneyNationalPark.com[2]**

**Just Add Courage!**

---

1. http://www.CCnDoc.com

2. http://www.MoneyNationalPark.com

**INSIDEOUT DISCOVERY™, INC.**
HOME OF COACHING FOR COMMITMENT
Just Add Courage!™

# About the Publisher

InsideOut Discovery™, Inc. (IOD) began as an International Organizational Development (OD) firm in 2002. Since then, it has grown into a holding company for a variety of different ventures including publishing.

IOD still operates as an OD firm providing executive coaching, leadership development, team building, and family governance; while its other brands vary from digital creation and storytelling to ebooks for kids of all ages and social media. For example, the CCnDoc brand is a personal look at an active over fifty lifestyle by two unapologetically eclectic influencers!

Published books include: *Coaching for Commitment Simplified, Courageous Money™: Your Adventure Through Money National Park™* and *The BIG Book of Southern Colorado Wildflowers: For kids of all ages.*

**www.InsideOutDiscovery.com**
**www.CCnDoc.com**
CCnDoc is an imprint of InsideOut Discovery, Inc.

Printed in the USA
CPSIA information can be obtained
at www.ICGtesting.com
LVHW010913061023
760263LV00037B/778